WHAT I ~~WISH~~
~~I HAD~~ KNOWN

WHAT I ~~WISH~~
~~I HAD~~ KNOWN

Laura Wiktorek

Laura Wiktorek

gatekeeper press
Columbus, Ohio

What I Wish I Had Known

Published by Gatekeeper Press
2167 Stringtown Rd, Suite 109
Columbus, OH 43123-2989
www.GatekeeperPress.com

Library of Congress Control Number: 2021941804

ISBN (paperback): 9781662915154
eISBN: 9781662915161

A Veteran's Prayer, Dedicated to my son,
Sgt. Michael Christopher Mead

Now I lay me down to sleep....

A veteran's prayer is what I keep

For post-traumatic stress relief.

Swollen eyes from tears I've cried

Always know you brought me pride

In more ways you'll ever know

In more ways, I could show.

PTSD can come and go

When it hits, we'll never know!

It takes twenty-two lives per day

One almost each hour to my dismay.

Serving your country, oh so well

Despite the fact that war is hell.

A veteran's world we'll never know

All the dark places you must go.

Memories of a war not left behind

Because they sit right in your mind.

So sorry that I missed the signs.

No words of wisdom did occur

To that you had to endure,

Those lost at war are far too many

Those lost at home even more plenty!

I can only hope you died not in vain,

but to help others who carry this pain.

ACKNOWLEDGMENTS

This memoir is dedicated to the men and women of the armed forces. The military community embraced me in my darkest hour. Thank you for your continued support. I found a sense of relief after Michael's former brothers-in-arms USMC Air Crew Chief Cpl. Erik Fries shared his recollection of war. It's the missing piece to this puzzling tragedy. Erik's brutal reply harshly described their Iraq experiences (his and Michael's), the gruesome painful details are precisely "what I wish I had known." I'd still be lingering in uncertainty. I thank you, Erik!

To Korah Hoffman, Michael's dear friend. When I reached out to you, I had no idea that you're a licensed therapist or how you would respond. Many years and miles have come between us. Your response was epic. I needed a stamp of approval from someone who loved and cherished Michael like me. You responded with solid professional, sound, and heartwarming advice. I treasure the wisdom and the friendship you shared with my daughter and son. Michael surrounded himself with loyal, selfless friends. Both you and Erik are a testament of that. I thank you, Korah!

To David Hazard (Ascent), my writing coach, editor/ mentor, and "therapist of sorts." The important message this memoir conveys would not be possible without your guidance, compassion, and empathy. I'm forever grateful for your assistance. Every time I was about to derail, you kept me on track. Thanks, David!

Thank you, Gatekeeper Press. I appreciate the talented staff you've provided me, and a special thanks to my Author Manager Eden Tuckman, you're awesome!

To Denise Lescano, medium/psychic, you provided me with much-needed solace and peace. Denise is a kind, caring soul with an exceptional gift that she shares with proficiency. Our encounter was life-changing. I thank you, Denise!

To my daughter Nikki and her husband, Scott, and my son Steve and his wife, Lauren alongside my six astonishing grandchildren, you provide me with purpose and unconditional love. I'm genuinely blessed and grateful. A special thanks to my friends Kari and Maria, and my sisters Mary and Susan. There are far too many to mention here, but you know who you are. Thank you for the encouraging words of wisdom and support. I'm grateful to have each and every single one of you in my life. Thank you all!

To Jenna Boyter, a truly amazing artist. Thank you for taking time out of your busy schedule to honor my son with the most exquisite butterfly tattoo. And a final shout out to Rachael Moses (Red Mar Photography). Thank you both!

CHAPTER 1

INSTINCTS

No parent carrying a newborn leaves the hospital with confidence, especially with their firstborn. Problems large and small present themselves from day one and throughout life. How we handle adversity is the evidence of what goes on in our subconscious mind. Don't ever underestimate that.

Most of my life, I've struggled to trust my instincts. As a result, I've learned the hard way that it's vital to nourish self-confidence. Problems never disappear if we disregard them. You have to trust yourself to recognize the signals coming in from those around you. While our misfortunes and mistakes have a price, we can learn, and we gain in wisdom from those costly experiences.

This is a costly story to tell.

With that said, I can tell you that the mistakes we make and the misfortunes we encounter mold us and make us who we are. Who I am – who I have become through these mistakes; I misread warning signs and signals from my son Michael before the darkness came –now, I'm someone much wiser than I was before this tragedy!

This book is the product of those experiences. Despite the darkness, I'm telling our story to offer you light and a way through.

Michael was born on Tuesday, March 9, 1982. I'd recently separated from my husband, Michael's father, in February of that year. Our marriage had been turbulent for a while, and we'd had an on-and-off relationship throughout the pregnancy. It was a challenging start to Michael's precious little life. When he was born, I was the ripe old age of nineteen and facing overwhelming circumstances. But, he was such a bundle of joy, and I was excited to welcome a son. I'd had Michael's sister, Nichole, in June of 1980, when I was just eighteen.

Life was filled with the joys of parenting two precious little ones. It was also a struggle, and I believe the distraction of trying to raise an infant and a toddler on my own set a pattern. This is not an excuse, but an explanation; my focus was constantly split, and I had to cling to hope, when circumstances were tough, that everything would somehow turn out alright.

I'd already gotten my GED and passed the state exams for my cosmetology license. I'd dropped out of high school and attended beauty school while pregnant. Nichole and Michael's father, who was four years older than me, had left town – which made my efforts at mothering much more difficult. I strived to improve our grim situation and held several jobs, trying to make ends meet. I was sleep-deprived, always on the go, and running on empty. We were barely getting by. Thankfully, I had a safety net that included an excellent support system in my parents and my sister Susan, and I was fortunate to live in an apartment just above their home. These circumstances were a blessing. I wouldn't have survived without them. The atmosphere fostered independence, yet family support was always nearby. As a result, Nichole and Michael established a close-knit relationship with my parents and with Susan. Still, turbulence erupted over and over throughout an ugly divorce, which dragged on for about a year and a half. At the time, it felt like forever. My ex was contesting; he insisted on trying to salvage the marriage. If that wasn't bad enough, we had a nasty custody battle that continued until he relocated to Kentucky.

Nikki and Michael's contact with their father dwindled over time, which I believe now, in hindsight, may have contributed to Michael's later tendency to do everything fiercely on his own without help.

Fortunately, the children's paternal grandparents stayed in touch, and as the kids grew, they continued to have an active relationship with them, celebrating their birthdays and holidays when the children were older, and sitting on the sidelines during sporting events to cheer them on. Their grandparents showed just as much pride in Nichole's and Michael's accomplishments as I did.

Here's where my mind goes back and forth. There were people to reach out to, people who loved Michael. Why didn't he? Why didn't he listen to the positive messages he'd heard all his life?

We're Catholic; I attended parochial school throughout elementary grades, but my children enrolled in public schools. They'd attended CCD classes at St. James Church, making their sacraments along the way. We attended weekly Mass, preferably on Saturday, but if Michael was serving on a Sunday, we'd visit the Mass he served. Michael was the only altar server in our home and had signed up on his own without my suggesting it. He made going to Mass at St. James a priority whenever he was in town. My mother was thoroughly convinced he would grow up to be a priest and expressed those sentiments many times over. Never once did he respond NO, which makes me wonder if he'd entertained the idea.

One thing is for sure. In our church, he was raised with life-affirming messages, and I was sure the religious upbringing was having a good effect on his character. You could witness it.

A typical summer weekend included a trip to my parents' permanent campground, just outside town. They owned a roomy newer trailer on Belden Hill. It was close enough to get to easily and far enough to call country. While young, the children often spent weekend overnights there with Susan and my parents. Typically, I'd work weekends in the fish store Mom had opened. My mother had started the business as a way to earn extra money to help support my handicapped sister Susan's speech therapy sessions. The kids kept amused with campfires, the pond, and eating s'mores. They'd gather branches from the surrounding woods to fuel the fire. It was a pleasant task that never got old or boring. Simply put, if there was a campfire, there was a marshmallow. And swimming in the pond, fishing, and catching newts were all part of the kids' youth.

Finally, our personal "weather forecast" changed to sunnier skies. I remarried in 1985 and moved in with my husband, Duane, just a few short blocks from my parents' home in Johnson City, New York. Nichole – Nikki – was five, and Michael was three. We were a package deal, and my new husband graciously accepted Nichole and Michael, and we became a happy family. Our son Steve was born the following summer in 1986. Duane took on the role of the level, calm parent, never the disciplinarian—that, he left that to me.

Our family felt complete. Stable and strong. Nikki and Michael started calling Duane "Dad" shortly after Steve was born. As early memories tend to develop around this time, he was their only constant father figure. By all accounts, he was and is their Dad. There was never a discussion about calling him Dad. They just did. The children played together as any siblings would. Steve, being so much younger, would interrupt an occasional board game, and Nikki had no patience for that. Michael was easygoing, but he loved to win.

I'm giving you these details for a reason.

The children spent plenty of time at Greens Field Park, one block from my parents' house, and just a few more from ours. At the park, they were exposed to arts and crafts and all sorts of athletic activities. They spent much of their time at the pool. They also relished their bikes and the independence their bikes gave them when they were a little older. They'd usually leave their bikes at my parents' place so they wouldn't have to drag them up our steep hill. In the winter, they enjoyed sledding and snowball fights.

What I'm saying is that our life had a stable base and was full of fun. That seemed to contribute to Michael's great sense of self-confidence – which sometimes put me on edge.

Michael was always drawn to adrenaline rushes and loved taking risks—the greater the risk, the greater the rush. He thoroughly enjoyed dangerous activities, including rock climbing and whitewater kayaking. He'd often do this with his biological father. He also enjoyed snowboarding and riding BMX bikes. He and his friend Jason moved massive amounts of earth to make some pretty impressive jumps! Later, he took up springboard diving, and that came with its own risks. I witnessed some pretty frightening results of his willingness to get creative off the diving board. He quickly learned that water isn't forgiving when your entry is off.

Still, I was proud of the young man he had become. His courage. His willingness to keep going until he mastered the next challenge. It was as if his spirit made him feel limitless.

I look back through the gray curtains of the more recent past, given my recurrent bouts of self-doubt, and second-guess: Did Michael feel loved? Part of a family that loved him? Where did the disconnect start?

I can come up with nothing but good memories, as do his siblings and grandparents. I would wonder later if Michael's can-do spirit would war against his care and concern for people when a very difficult call had to be made. I'd describe us as a fairly typical, American, blended family. Later, when I would have to search my soul for answers, I could find no signs of instability or lack of support here.

What I am left with is the belief that Michael's early and growing-up years gave him a stable base mentally, spiritually, and in terms of family relationships.

What went wrong? And when? These are questions that drive me to comb the later years and experiences, looking for answers as to why I lost my son and what I can tell others, hoping to help them avoid the same painful tragedy. Starting with this advice: *trust your instincts.*

CHAPTER 2

GROWING UP QUICK

From changing diapers to high school open house, lickety-split teenagers evolved. Early on, I vividly recall a phone conversation I received from Mr. V, one of Michael's elementary teachers. He wanted permission for Michael to stay in on his lunch break. Michael expressed an interest in designing a game for a classmate with special needs because Matthew was confined to a wheelchair with limited use of his limbs. "Yes, of course," I agreed happily. When we hung up, I had to smile. Michael was a kind, gentle soul, empathetic beyond his years. It took days, but his well-thought plan produced a game that Matthew could play. This was another example of how positive the influence my sister Susan has.

Michael & Matthew

I'm confident dad's (grandpa's) carpentry skills and natural mechanics contributed to some of Michael's keen attributes. One of Michael's earliest gifts was a toolbox, complete with a hammer and nails, screws and screwdrivers, and not to mention plenty of fresh-cut wood to practice. He was building things with my dad as a toddler. Both grandfathers played positive roles, impacting Michael.

Michael was at ease with people. He played cards with his grandmother and her two best friends, Madge and Sally, for hours on end. He enjoyed their company just as much as he enjoyed playing with the kids, and mom, Sally, and Madge thoroughly enjoyed his. He'd play with children older and younger, gifted or handicapped, and he'd have a good time with anyone. Michael's connection to everyone around him was not limited to people. He was gentle with animals, too. We had an energetic boxer named Ginger, a huge 125-gallon aquarium full of creatures, turtles, and Rocky, our iguana, not to mention Peanut Butter and Jelly, our cockatiels.

Michael showed his kindness by going above and beyond. He cleared our elderly neighbor's snowy driveway without being asked. If he saw something that needed to be done, he'd do it. He'd stop playing a game of kickball to help with groceries and changed many stranger's tires on the road. I can't tell you how many times he came into the house filthy after helping someone whose car had broken down. The kind of guy even a stranger could count on, a guardian angel of sorts.

Again, in hindsight, it's also possible that Michael's deeper nature, his kindness and love for people, would work against him later in life when painful memories of war and an incident for which he held himself responsible would come back to haunt him.

I'm painting a picture of Michael as an "angel child," I know. I won't paint an inaccurate picture. Michael may have been spiritual, but he enjoyed spirits, too. As he grew up, I'm sure he did his share of overindulging in drink. He worked hard, but he also played hard. His high school yearbook quote is, "Where's the party? Ski club, swim team & track." His "Notable" was "Party Animal!" Thankfully, he outgrew that distinction.

What I learned to cling to in the midst of child-rearing struggles were the good times. I leaned into the good and sweet and wonderful, always maintaining a positive focus.

Michael wasn't an only child. It's essential to share the lives that surrounded him.

Nikki and Mike spent a lot of time together; I suppose their close age fostered a friendship. They enjoyed snowboarding and BMX tournaments, and they shared many close friends. Two years after she graduated, Nikki enthusiastically attended Michael's prom with Vince, a close friend of Michael's. They'd attended prom in a big group. Nikki and Michael happened to share a best friend, Korah. She also attended prom in this large group. Nikki was the only high school graduate. There is no doubt in my mind that Nikki enjoyed being a part of Michael's prom much more than she had her own.

As a teen, Nichole sometimes sported odd hair colors– pink, green, blue–she even shaved her head once or twice along the way. She shopped at thrift stores long before they were the thing to do. She's a trend setter with a distinct taste. Nikki expressed herself through pottery and art, incredibly creative and naturally gifted in athletics and the arts. In high school, she clearly stood out on the cheerleading squad (only a handful of girls were gymnasts). She excelled in springboard diving, as well. Strong-willed, at times challenging, perhaps because she's the oldest, although I have a strong feeling it wouldn't matter where she landed in the lineup, she entertained the notion that she's the black sheep. It couldn't be farther from the truth. Contrary to her self-image, her quirky personality is what I love and adore. Brutally honest… what you see is what you get!

I'll never forget when Nikki wanted to introduce her new boyfriend to her grandmother. "Gram, I want you to know I'm dating a tattoo artist." Mom replied, "What does that mean? Does he have a tattoo?" Nikki replied, "No, Gram, he is a tattoo!" Such a nice guy, he wanted to marry her, but he wasn't the one. To this day, I chuckle when I think about it. I was impressed that Nikki walked away from the relationship without a single tattoo. They'd come much later.

Growing up, Michael and Steve shared a bedroom. Steve resembled his dad, long and lean. Both boys sported short hair, clean cut. Unlike Michael, Steve wasn't the least bit shy. Steve's gregarious; he'd make friends remarkably easy. Exhibiting confidence, yet thoughtful and caring. Steve rarely studied but maintained excellent grades. He was enrolled in advanced classes. Nikki worked hard to attain high-honor roll; Michael fell somewhere in the middle during his high school years. When it came to college, Michael soared to academic excellence. Although Michael was the middle child, without a doubt, both siblings looked up to him.

The boys were born four years apart. By the time Steve was in eighth grade, he was competing in three varsity sports:

golf, wrestling, and track. It was Michael's senior year, making them track teammates. Just like Michael, Steve is an outstanding athlete striving to hit or beat any and every milestone Michael had. Michael wholeheartedly encouraged him. Steve's wrestling team earned a NY State Championship title. Just like Michael, Steve competed at the state level in multiple sports, setting new school records along the way. Steve was instantly popular. After all, his senior teammates were friends with Michael.

Among the three, there were tons of activities, and they were all competitive. Duane and I often sat on separate sidelines calling each other to see how competition was going on the other side. We traveled to many destinations, commonly involving competition with gymnastics, Taekwondo, golf, and wrestling. We trekked to tournaments in Florida, Illinois, Kentucky, Virginia, and even Las Vegas. Nikki and Michael flew to Fort Lauderdale for a week or two of diving camp, and that eliminated any vacation budget. We spent a heap of time and money visiting a good portion of states throughout the years. At one point, all three children and I were enrolled in Taekwondo. They were some of the best days of my life.

CHAPTER 3

RECRUITED

Where does anyone's sense of certainty, focus, and drive come from?

Michael contemplated joining the military long before he graduated from high school, certain that was the right direction for him. He not only engaged in discussions with recruiters, but he also participated full-speed ahead in their timed competitions. Apparently, they were impressed, and soon after his success in the competitions, calls started pouring in, and recruiters were banging down the door. On the written exams, Michael scored in the highest range, and his athletic abilities were visibly above average. The enthusiastic recruiters reassured him that he could have any job he desired within the Corps if he signed early. They assured Michael and me that signing early had perks, such as less call-back time after he served full term. Call-back time would be subtracted from the amount of time for which he originally signed. He would also have the opportunity to choose what field he'd work in.

Once he expressed interest to the recruiters, who seemed to be everywhere, the pressure on Michael was relentless. True, he was eager to sign up, but at this point, he was only seventeen. It was late September, and he wouldn't be eighteen until March and graduating from high school in late June. Hearing him talk about the relentless pursuit of the recruiters, I thought, *What's the hurry?*

The pressure troubled me enough that I let Michael and the recruiters know exactly how I felt, and I tried to ignore the constant push for my signature. The fact is, Michael was relentless. When he wanted something, there was no stopping him. His persistence was nonstop.

"Mom, please, if you don't sign, I'm going to anyway when I'm eighteen, and then I'll probably get some crappy job or assignment. They're offering me my choice right here, right now!"

This perpetual plea went on for weeks, clearly trying to break me down.

Here was my weak point. Michael rarely asked for anything. He made everyone feel important and was always willing to help around the house every time I asked and even when I didn't. He would never complain about any task. Because he rarely asked for favors, it was hard to deny him this one request. Besides, my parenting philosophy was this–

As parents, we supervise, steering our children toward positive paths. Eventually, we need to let go and trust the skills we taught them. They need to decide what path to take. Instead of thinking about all the reasons you think they shouldn't choose something, look at things from their perspective; maybe then it will make sense. After all, I had learned more from my mistakes, much more than any lessons that came from success, and I'd had more than my fair share of blunders. It's okay to have hopes and dreams for your children; it's not okay to steal or deny theirs.

Still, I was reluctant to meet the recruiter. I certainly have nothing against the military. I admire and respect all service members. My rationale that day was my motherly instinct. Going through my head were thoughts such as, *I don't want my son shot, or for that matter, have him shooting anyone.*

I asked Michael, "How are you going to kill someone?" Michael wasn't a hunter; he was a gentle soul.

His tenacity was steadfast, though, and he kept insisting that I sit down with recruiters. I finally did. Michael made the arrangements, and soon a man in uniform, a sergeant in the Marines, was sitting at my kitchen table.

A lengthy discussion ensued. I made sure to express my concerns about the probability of war loud and clear. Of course, the recruiter had all the right answers.

"Mrs. Wiktorek, there's always a possibility of reinstating the draft, and in that case, there'll be no say in the matter." He made it clear that if someone is drafted, they no longer had a choice, and he insinuated that in the case of war, Michael's odds/fate could include the front line. As it turned out, he'd more or less signed up for that. At least now, he was offered an opportunity to choose.

I could tell this guy knew what he was doing, never rushing, patiently sustaining his military case. He appealed to my sense of patriotism and pointed out that other parents were allowing their children to join. I didn't question his integrity, because to me, that's what the Marines stand for. Michael and the recruiter prevailed by double-teaming me. I didn't want to crush Michael's dreams, and I gave in despite my unwavering fears.

I'm a pushover. I trust everyone and take them at their word. I would one day realize it's a flaw of mine. Somehow, I always trust others. Why didn't I believe in myself and listen to intuition?

As long as I live, I'll never forget the gut-wrenching feeling I had right before signing. It was an overwhelming, unsettling intuition, perhaps a warning that my son would go to war and that I'd bury him. I should have listened to it, and I learned from this incident to do just that. Now I know that even if someone is pushing you to do something you're unsure of, trust your instinct and don't do it. I'd had a similar, eerie feeling one other time, right before signing for my first marriage license. Deep down, I knew our marriage would never last, but we had Nichole, so I wanted to try. The marriage didn't end well. But we had Michael, so something good came from it.

The eerie feeling I had sitting in the kitchen with Michael and the recruiter had a much stronger pull. The thought of war paralyzed me with a horrible feeling of terror. My intuition was telling me no, but my son was begging me to sign, clearly tugging at my heartstrings. Michael's father would also need to sign. They contacted him in Kentucky, and he made sure they put their promises in writing. He always thought things out, while I, on the other hand, surrendered myself to overwhelming emotions. Finally, I signed the parental consent form, and the sergeant left.

Immediately, I broke down and cried, shouting, "I'm going to bury my son!"

Then I headed straight to my bedroom, tears streaming down my face.

My memories of that day are crystal clear. Michael charged after me and stood in the bedroom doorway. I heard a gentle chuckle, not the mocking kind.

"Mom, thanks. But don't worry about me. It's going to be okay. Everything is going to be fine. There's not going to be a war. I'm not going to war! I'm not going to die. I'm just going into the military."

He continued to chuckle as he gently closed the door. I lay there, sobbing, and my mind raced to the worst-case scenarios. I felt as though I had just made the biggest mistake of my life. I just wanted what's best for Michael, and I loved him so much.

Michael was going to be a Marine! At his diving state debut, college coaches approached him about attending their schools, but the deal was already sealed. He was going into the Marine Corps and wouldn't be attending college or pursuing any of his athletic abilities. I couldn't help but think that if I made him wait to sign on his own after he turned eighteen, perhaps he might have changed his mind. He could have decided to dive or run in college. He wasn't yet eighteen and was doing dives he'd never tried before. His trademark dive was a backward dive, two and a half twists, one flip rotation, in the straight position, a 2.7 degree of difficulty. I don't ever remember seeing any other diver do that dive. He'd been doing it for years. I never understood how he knew when to stop twisting. A 2.0 DD, when executed correctly, brought in high scores, and 3.0 was the cap for DD at that time. But it didn't matter. His destiny was determined, even though he was diving better than ever and college coaches were interested in signing him. Michael ran the 800 in two minutes flat, qualifying him for states. Only a handful of students earned the honor of bearing their name on the high school marquee: "Good Luck at States." It's located at the entrance and exit of the high school. Michael earned that honor multiple times.

Immediately after his high school graduation ceremony, Michael was rushed by a recruiter, who confiscated his high school diploma right there on the spot as we exited the building.

I was shocked. In that moment, the reality of the military was sinking in. Michael didn't say much; I honestly think he was shocked, as well. Fortunately, the recruiter didn't take Michael along with his diploma, and we were able to celebrate his graduation with family and friends. As usual, Michael's paternal grandparents were present, and his father also made the trip to celebrate his graduation.

It was only a short time before the Marines came and swept Michael off to boot camp. The date was preset but, with very little notice, it was moved up. The Marine Corps would be calling the shots for Michael for the next five years. Since he signed on to be an aircrew chief, he needed an additional year of service on top of the usual required four years. When it was time to go, they picked him up right at the house. Nikki showed up early to say her goodbyes.

Michael promised to call me as soon as he got to boot camp, but he didn't.

It felt to me as if the Marines were quickly cutting all ties with his family. Now, they "owned" him.

He did write to us, though. In one letter, he indicated that he was excelling athletically at boot camp. I wasn't surprised because I was confident in his abilities to excel there. In fact, he mentioned the possibility of making Ironman status, which is an honor conferred on the top athlete in the class of graduating recruits. If he earned it, his reward would be to automatically jump rank. It was a very big deal. His running skills complemented his endurance. It turns out those are highly desirable assets at boot camp. The years of sports and gymnastics in which he'd participated gave him strength and agility.

Later, he reported this–when the final physical fitness test took place, it was a sweltering day. Parris Island is scorching in the summer. Soaking in sweat while completing chin-ups, he ultimately lost his grip and slipped off the bar. He was so close, but a chin-up or two cost him the honor of Ironman. Michael was never a show-off, nor did he ever brag. It just wasn't his style. When he told us the results, he still sounded confident in his athletic abilities.

Michael was still growing when he entered the Marine Corps. The Corps lined up recruits by height, and they kept adjusting his place in line as he grew so that, ultimately, he moved up about eight slots in the lineup. Some guys had food rations, but Michael was given extra portions to help him grow and gain weight. Hence, the big guys became his chow buddies.

Later, too, he told us stories about boot camp and the Crucible Confidence Course. Every Marine is required to get through this physical and mental challenge that takes place in the heart of the woods, demanding a march on foot for forty-five miles. Both food and sleep deprivation are part of this challenge. The Crucible warranted completion within about two days. Michael said he'd helped carry a fellow recruit in a reenactment of a casualty. Of course, they'd never pick him to be the casualty; he was way too small. He said they chose the biggest guys to be carried.

I was very impressed with what he endured.

If I had worried about Michael's character changing when he became a Marine, that was wasted energy.

At boot camp, he had decided to continue his childhood role as an altar server, indicating he'd developed a friendly relationship with the chaplain on base. My mother was so pleased to hear the news. I vividly recall attending Mass on boot camp graduation weekend. The church was packed. I honestly couldn't believe it.

Michael smiled at me and said, "Mom, it's the only place you can go in boot camp where you can't get yelled at. *Everyone* goes to church." Some young men were asleep in the pews, while others were visibly crying.

When asked about the tears, Michael shared the sad news: a young man had committed suicide that weekend. He'd hung himself in the restroom on base.

Again, my fears returned. I had detected that circumstances were extremely tough, but I didn't expect that anyone would die during basic training, and I thought of the five years Michael had ahead of him.

Michael continued training for an Air Crew Chief position, now stationed at Camp Lejeune in North Carolina, where he would establish lifelong bonds. I remember the day this small, elite group graduated. My parents and I drove from upstate New York to North Carolina for this special occasion. I'll never forget seeing the massive CH53 Super Stallion helicopter and hearing the commanding officer's powerful and compelling speech. It went something like this:

> These young Marine Corps earned their wings alongside the title Air Crew Chief to the CH53

Super Stallion Helicopter. This mammoth machine is large enough to transport a military tank, valued as an intricate tool, and revered with monumental importance. The safety of every flight falls on these young Marine Corps. Pilots count on this; their lives depend on it. Every flight consists of two pilots and two enlisted aircrew members. Proper inspection is imperative to ensure safety; otherwise, crew and cargo are in jeopardy. They carry the future of our Corps. Not only do they have the tremendous job of serving and maintaining this colossal piece of equipment, but their shoulders bear the heavy burden that comes with the immense responsibility/accountability of transporting our most treasured cargo, the Marine Corps themselves! The maximum capacity for this giant machine is fifty-five passengers.

USMC Erik Fries & Michael Mead

I was astonished, not just by the hard work Michael put in, but at the fact that, at nineteen, my young son was part of this elite group, with such immense responsibilities! I was incredibly proud. I'm not sure he fully understood what he signed up for. I certainly didn't until that moment. The Marine Corps had tremendous confidence in these young Marines. They'd earned their wings. It was unusual for Marines to train together and go on to serve together — but they would be stationed together. A brotherhood in arms is about to grow strong. They were now family away from family.

After boot camp and Air Crew Chief training, Michael had even more intense training instructions. He continued practical training in Pensacola, Florida, and sent pictures depicting an indoor pool crash simulator. Crash training involved quickly exiting the aircraft while underwater. He would also be dropped out of a helicopter and plunged into the bitter cold, rough ocean to tread water in the frigid temperatures for hours on end. Another aspect of training included a parachute drag, where he was continuously dragged in the cold water until he could successfully get out of the parachute. Around that time, the group thinned out a bit. It was an intense exercise, not just mentally but physically, and not everyone could handle it. My assumption was that they were making sure these young warriors had survival skills to overcome a crash landing, especially in water.

Once training was complete, Michael and his comrades were stationed in San Diego, California, at Miramar Naval Base. This was his permanent station (unless deployed) for the duration of his service. Of course, at the time, he didn't know that. Michael drove from upstate New York to California and met his buddy and comrade Erik in St. Louis on the road.

Unfortunately, the trip was delayed when Michael discovered he left his military dress uniform behind in Kentucky when he'd made a pit stop to visit his father along the way. He wasn't about to show up without it! His buddy Erik waited while Michael drove back to retrieve it. Other than backtracking, I think he enjoyed this road trip and was excited to have a permanent station. He was ready, willing, and able to launch enthusiastically into his new military ventures. I envisioned him staying in California, enjoying the west coast, the ocean, the mountains.

Fate was about to throw us a curveball.

On September 11, 2001, like everyone else, I was glued to the TV and radio. Everyone was confused about what was happening and why. Once the news confirmed that it was a terrorist attack, I knew my son's future; after all, he was a Marine. I relived signing the parental consent form, and thoughts of war were naturally triggered. My mind was racing with fear.

Without wasting any time, I purchased the next available airline tickets for a flight to San Diego. Nichole and I flew out of Newark, New Jersey, to California directly after 9/11. Airline tickets were dirt cheap—after all those airline crashes, nobody wanted to fly. We bought the first flight out of Newark.

Nikki and I were going to California to be with Michael. We knew he would be going to war; it was just a matter of time.

CHAPTER 4

9/11

The terrorist attack that brought down the World Trade Center's Twin Towers sent a terrible, painful shock through America and the world.

One positive thing that was about to happen in our private world, at least, offering us a small bright spot in the midst of a great, national tragedy, was that Nikki and I would pay Michael a visit.

When we flew from Newark to California to visit Michael, airport security was grueling; every safeguard was in place. When we arrived in San Diego, the Naval Base was on high alert: color code orange.

Despite the grim reality of 9/11, we decided to make the best of our time together. It was clear the Marines were mobilizing for war. We visited SeaWorld, taking immense pleasure in the beautiful aquatic displays. Mike took Nikki and me rock climbing. He started us out slow on a small boulder, at least in comparison to those in our backdrop. Nikki held her own, but I wasn't feeling it; I'm afraid of heights. I suppose there's a first time for everything, but for me, this was my first and last rock climbing. We also savored some of Michael's favorite local eateries and one night ate at the Hard Rock Café.

Then came a pleasant surprise. Michael was promoted while we were there, and we attended the simple ceremony. Nichole and I had the honor of pinning Michael's chevrons on his shoulders, Nikki on one shoulder, and I on the other. We were thrilled to be present to see Michael promoted to Lance Corporal.

Nichole, Michael & Laura

We knew he would deploy – it was inevitable after the grim reality of 9/11. Had I known it wasn't going to be immediate, I might have waited to fly out to visit him later. Nonetheless, we spent quality time together on that trip and got a unique look at life on base and at Michael in his military environment.

Michael went on to spend a significant segment training in the desert. As a tactics and weapon instructor, he would soon start training Marines himself. He told us he trained with night vision, and I suspect his training involved being a door gunner, which is when a soldier shoots a gun directly from the open door of the helicopter. After all, they were heading off to war. That's not the kind of information Michael shared; he tried to make light of things. I'm sure after all the fuss I made about war, he was shielding me from some of the truth. That still haunts me.

What I know now is the importance of being a non-anxious presence for your sons and daughters – the calm, listening parent with whom they can share anything. I wish I had been more of that kind of parent for Michael; instead, I realize that because he'd witnessed me fall apart, he was always trying to protect me from hard realities.

Like any typical military member, Michael missed out on many life-changing events, not to mention umpteen holidays! Once, while he was home on leave, we gathered around the kitchen table, and my mother-in-law kept looking at Michael and Steve. She glanced back and forth, and suddenly she blurted out, "If I didn't know any better, I'd think you two were brothers!" We chuckled, but it wasn't funny. The reality was that she was experiencing dementia. We were aware that she'd been slipping, but that comment demonstrated just how severe her memory loss was. She came to live with us after that.

Eventually, the day arrived when Michael deployed to Iraq. He left in August 2004 and returned in March 2005. While his deployment was only about eight months, it felt like an eternity. The tragic, traumatic events that culminated during his deployment destroyed many families. The devastating loss of life traumatized so many, not to mention those who served beside them.

During his deployment, we heard from him from time to time – phone calls, an occasional letter. Of course, there was little he could discuss or divulge of a military nature, and given the roughness of Marine life amid the great difficulties of war in Iraq, he spared us the details.

If I thought at all about him shielding us from difficult truths, I accepted that as normal. How was I to guess that keeping things about his experience secret was forming not only a bad habit – that of keeping a barrier between himself and everyone else when it came to working through stresses and emotional hardships?

One of the deadliest incidents in the Iraq war occurred during Michael's deployment. He never shared his personal side of these painful experiences, and I only later learned of his peripheral involvement. His duty was to write the flight schedule for an ill-fated flight.

Tragic, traumatic events that occurred during this war hurt and even destroyed many families, not only those directly involved, but for those who served beside the fallen.

News came on January 26, 2005, about a terrible accident and the loss of American lives.

I heard the breaking news at dinner time from the kitchen: "A helicopter crashed in Iraq."

I ran from the kitchen to the TV in the family room, frantic. My husband said calmly. "It was a group of Marines out of Hawaii." Still, my heart was pounding. Once you're part of the greater military family, every loss hurts.

The news broadcast resumed. They confirmed a transporting helicopter; CH-53E Super Stallion crashed in Iraq.

My mind raced. *That's Michael's helicopter. It's his machine!*

Again, Duane assured me. "It can't be Michael. If it were, they'd be saying the troops were out of San Diego. They're not."

The TV reporters kept repeating that the Marines were Hawaii-based. They're still uncovering information.

Michael called that evening, obviously shaken, his voice somber. I detected a quiver in his words as he stumbled through what he told us. Never in my life had I heard him sound so upset and unsettled.

"Mom, I'm calling to let you know I'm okay. I wasn't on that flight. Everything's okay. There was a crash. It wasn't me. I'm fine. But I'm in a hurry. I don't have time to talk."

"I love you," I blurted into the phone, trying not to cry – even in relief.

The conversation ended abruptly. On one hand, I was relieved for us – though devastated by the loss of life. So many parents were learning their loved ones were gone. Dead. On the other, I felt uneasy about the sound of Michael's voice. I could tell he was deliberately avoiding offering us any details, maybe because they were secret or maybe to ease my mind. He had made it sound like he wasn't anywhere near that crash site.

When it came to his service, Michael was very secretive. Everything was classified, and he would never divulge the details of duty - where he was going, where he was. He would flat-out say, "I can't talk about that."

I wondered if all military personnel live by this "can't talk" code of ethics. I came to understand that it's necessary during wartime, to keep important information from leaking to the enemy and endangering missions and lives. But what about after? I wonder if, then, it's a way to avoid painful conversation.

Only years later would I learn about the events of that fateful day. Fateful for the troops that died, of course, but fateful for Michael and for us, too.

January 26, 2005, a transport helicopter crashed in Western Iraq, killing a total of 31 men. The CH-53E Super Stallion Helicopter carried 26 Hawaii-based Marines and five additional members (four Marines, one Navy medic).

The coalition was trying to secure the country ahead of the Iraq parliamentary election slated to take place later that month. The enemy could have called it the perfect storm; Iraq forces were pressuring, our military responded with night flights, which also forced them to maneuver closer to ground. That in itself poses a huge risk.

The Super Stallion is the largest military helicopter. The determined cause of the crash was complicated, combining several factors. Pilots were becoming disorientated during that time as they flew into a sandstorm. Since the weather was terrible, that added torque to the equipment. Combine that with a heavy load of personnel, and the outcome was dire. They also suspected errors were made using night vision.

The result was one of the deadliest crashes in U.S. military history.

Among the multitude of misfortunes was the fact – which we also learned much later – that Michael assigned the flight schedule that evening. Michael, the line chief, decided to swap out a more experienced crew member for a less experienced aircrew chief. He did so to offer the more experienced guy some much-needed respite for the long hours he'd been called on to work and from the fatigue of war. The aircrew chief on board was new to the field, a rookie of sorts. He wasn't new to the Corps, just to that field. For that matter, their flight-crew command team, Michael's group, was overworked, drained, sleep-deprived, and under immense pressure. They desperately needed time off or even just good night's sleep. As it was – we learned – the military gives out uppers to keep personnel awake during high-stress, high-demand times, adding to mental disorientation. Imagine waking up in the middle of a combat nightmare, on high alert, with critical demands being made of you.

If you're a pilot or aircrew chief, it doesn't get any worse than this.

Despite being in a war zone with all its chaos, Michael tried his best to call home and give us whatever details about himself and his well-being as he was allowed to share. He knew his family was worried, as were his friends. He told us that lines for the phones were long on holidays but that he didn't mind waiting, and I'm incredibly grateful for every call.

What I couldn't see was the invisible wall that was being erected between what Michael was thinking and experiencing from all of us who loved him.

Meanwhile, there were distractions here at home. Together with my parents, I was busy in a tropical fish store – business was booming, an unexpected success – and that took up hours of time and careful attention. On top of that, I had a beauty salon to run out of my home, with plenty of clients to serve.

A barrage of health issues also demanded attention. My husband's kidneys were failing, and he needed another transplant. He'd already had one transplant, a kidney that lasted over twenty years. I'd assumed it would last forever, but that wasn't the case. Back in the '80s, only blood relatives would be considered as donors; the technology wasn't there to test potential donors outside the family. Now, we jump-started the transplant process in hopes of avoiding dialysis. Since I'm the same blood type, we tested to see if I was a match and scheduled an evaluation at Upstate Medical Center in Syracuse, New York. Duane's first transplant was done there, and it's only an hour from home. After his blood work and evaluation, they revealed that they weren't going to be able to transplant. Unfortunately, they had discovered Hep C, so Duane was considered high-risk. We were completely shocked. He'd received blood transfusions every time he went to dialysis in the '80s, which took place three days a week for well over a year. Back then, blood banks didn't check for Hep C or HIV, so it shouldn't have been a shock, but it was.

So, Michael was at war, and my husband's health was on a steady decline; the prognosis was bleak. His doctors proceeded with arrangements, seeking a high-risk transplant center. Eventually, I'd be deemed a match for my husband's much-needed transplant.

I only relate these details to say, in almost everyone's life, there are huge demands. It is easy to miss distress signals from someone – even a loved one – who is struggling, especially if they downplay or minimize their own troubles. Life throws us all too much to handle sometimes. That is simply part of our too often tragic human condition–difficult to accept, maybe, but an important piece of the truth.

While going through all this, I started to make two "welcome home" banners. Michael's deployment was nearing an end. Prayers were said that no tragedies would prevent him from returning safely home. Focusing on the banners was something positive I could do during this difficult and chaotic time.

On one, I stenciled in bold letters: "Welcome Home Sgt. Michael Mead." The fabric for that one was military khaki canvas, and I stitched two symbols on it: a Flying Tiger patch and a USMC patch; the second banner a solid green with a huge yellow "THANK YOU!" On that one, I tied a yellow ribbon for every day Michael spent in Iraq; it was full of yellow ribbons. I added red and blue for the days he was back on U.S. soil but not home yet.

Now, I was counting down the days to Michael's homecoming. We had the holidays to get through; I'd put together a "home for the holidays" scrapbook, jammed full with pages from family and friends. I encouraged everyone to use their imagination and do whatever inspired them, and the result was an incredible, unique glimpse into what was happening at home. The scrapbook was full of wonderful expressions of encouragement and comments about how grateful we were for his service and sacrifice. My cousin, a teacher in New Jersey, had each of her elementary students write personal letters to Michael.

When he received them, he called to say how much he enjoyed this gift. He thoroughly enjoyed the loving wishes of family and friends and the innocent and honest notes from the grade-schoolers. Words of encouragement meant the world to him.

When he touched down on U.S. soil, I sighed with relief. Unfortunately, there was no way I could travel to meet his plane.

I was administering peritoneal dialysis to Duane and was caring for my mother-in-law. That is sometimes the way life goes, isn't it? We have more to do, more to care about, and far more than we can handle.

Once, my mother-in-law wandered off from our home. I was working at the tropical fish store when the police called Duane to come to get her. She'd been apprehended for shoplifting, but it was clear she had no idea she hadn't paid for the items.

I was also taking care of my grandson, Dante, while working two jobs, just as I had with my children while they were growing up.

All I could do was wait for Michael's return to home territory.

On May 2, 2005, my mother and I drove to the Syracuse Airport to pick Michael up. We proudly held up his welcome home banner, and as he made his way through the terminal, everybody around us stopped and start clapping and cheering! I'll never forget his reaction. For a split second, he acted like he didn't know us. He pulled his chin in, then slightly shook his head *no*.

I took this as a sign that he didn't want any fuss about him or his return. That he didn't want to call attention to himself. In time, it would occur to me that maybe he was also trying to leave behind something he did not want to remember.

I was crying, of course, tears of joy and relief, and I'm pretty sure my mother cried, too. When I finally embraced him, it hands down topped the list of most significant moments in my life. An awesome wave of relief washed over me, seeing and holding him. I felt pride, love, happiness—you name it. It had been so long since I'd smiled and really felt it.

His welcome home party was around the corner on Friday, and I could finally put to rest all those silly worries about burying my son.

If there were changes in Michael – a little more quiet/ reflective, an occasional tendency to isolate himself – they are noticeable only in hindsight, really. Maybe his time in the service, with its weight of responsibilities, had just deepened him.

I didn't take them as signs – as I might have – that more was going on inside Michael than any of us knew. And there were so many life details to catch up on.

When we pulled up to the house, one of my huge banners hung high, right beside the American flag. The enormous green banner with all those yellow ribbons, sporting a gigantic yellow "THANK YOU!" waved proudly on our front porch. This time when Michael spotted it, he chuckled with a great big smile.

As for me, I wanted life from now on to be great for him.

Our welcome home celebration was at the Knights of Columbus. We had a great turnout. So many people from the community had supported us while Michael was in Iraq. The local news stations even checked in to see how he was doing. Everyone was thrilled to see Michael, and we had plenty of food and fun, with tons of red, white, and blue balloons and other decorations. As usual, Michael's paternal grandparents came, but his father wasn't able to attend. I hired a minuteman; he arrived dressed as a Revolutionary War soldier and rang a bell while proclaiming, "Hear ye, hear ye!" As he started a clever poem, it progressed into a song based on Michael's life experiences. Our local Action News was there; a former swim teammate was the cameraman. It felt like everything was going back to the way it used to be.

Only during his interview did a very somber moment arise, when Michael described a devastating crash during his tour. He said that not a day went by that he didn't reflect on those who didn't make it home alive.

"...not a day goes by...."

I heard those words but didn't take into account what they really meant, which was that a dark inner path had opened up in my son's soul.

Soon after, Michael shared a solemn photograph taken in Iraq showing a gun resting in empty combat boots. On top of the gun sat a helmet. The photo depicted a somber final salute. That was just one of many missed opportunities to intervene. Michael indicated that the official determination of the crash the photo referred to was vertigo or perhaps weather; he made a derogatory comment about how they always blame the pilot. I wasn't sure what he meant. I knew the helicopters were old, and sometimes parts were obsolete. I don't think he ever actually used the words "bubble gum" or "duct tape," but he somehow gave the impression that something like that was used to repair the helicopters. When you're smack in the middle of a war, you make do.

Looking back on those incidents, I feel ashamed. I berated myself, saying I should have paid closer attention. I was trying to balance personal responsibilities and struggles along with plans and just the joy of Michael's return. At that moment in time, that's all I cared about.

Later, I would have my own inner battle to fight. It would make me sick to think I was that thoughtless and missed cues. I'd punish myself mentally for being so "insensitive" and "selfish."

I would have to learn that beating yourself up does no one any good.

Then again, at other times, I realize that military personnel are trained to wall off their feelings in order to be good Marines/soldiers. There is no time in the midst of battle to give in to emotions. Afterwards, it's hard to open up and revisit feelings you've buried in order to survive. I believe this mindset is behind so many post-combat veteran breakdowns and even worse tragedies.

All that mattered to me at the time was that Michael was honorably discharged after his five years of service. Finally home and eager to start college, he took the SAT exam in preparation for enrolling in college. He wasn't sure where he'd land, but his heart was set on an architecture program. The University of Buffalo, New York, was his first choice. Because he'd been out of school for five years, they required him to take pre-math courses along with some basic classes before launching into the actual architecture program, and that added an extra year. It would eat up grants, but it would be beneficial.

We still had a little time left to summer before he moved to Buffalo. He had started dating a pretty blonde with beautiful bright blue eyes, Leia. They'd went to JC High School together. She graduated a year behind Michael. Leia had a sweet little girl, the same age as Dante, my grandson. Michael adored them both. He quickly fell in love with Leia. It was a whirlwind romance, and in a matter of months, they were engaged. Then, as quickly as their relationship started, it ended. At that point, it was a long-distance relationship; she was in Johnson City while he was in Buffalo.

Michael still seemed somewhat broken-hearted the following summer, but as usual, he didn't share his feelings. I just knew he wasn't happy.

Sometimes there was a distant look on his face. A sense of gray gloominess. If asked what was wrong, he was too quick to say, "nothing." At the same time, his pace of life picked up, and he was in constant motion. Some say he may have been running from his emotions, but he had always been intense. It really wasn't out of character for Michael to stay extremely active.

Again, I focused on his future, hoping that whatever small shadows I saw would vanish in the apparent brightness of what lay ahead.

He had college to look forward to; he was finally entering the architecture program. Once college resumed, there wasn't going to be any free time. Michael indicated he'd be up all night, finishing projects. We knew he'd be extremely busy because he was determined to reach and maintain a 4.0 GPA. An article in the UB news listed the architect program as the hardest undergraduate program they offered at the time, which made his GPA even more impressive.

His drive to succeed did seem a little over the top – but then again, that was Michael, the overachiever.

Life threw more distractions: Not long after Duane's kidney transplant, my mother developed breast cancer and would need a mastectomy as soon as possible. Not only that—my father needed a heart defibrillator. He had already rescheduled his surgery because of the transplant. After mom's diagnosis, it would be pushed back a little longer. I went back to work in the store shortly after my surgery. I was moving slower than usual, but I managed.

This whole scenario seemed to be typical for our family; we could never have one crisis at a time. My guess is that it's like this for many families. Life can be like trying to herd wild horses. Good luck keeping up with all of it.

Sometime around fall of that year, Michael met a beautiful woman named Kristina at the University of Buffalo, and in the spring, he brought her home. Kristina was lovely and genuinely sweet. She also seemed shy. Later it occurred to me that she was a lot like Michael. She passed the dog test. Usually, whenever we'd have company, they'd be afraid of our large bullmastiff, Abby. Kristina wasn't nervous around her at all, and Abby never left her side. I didn't realize how young Kristina was until much later because she seemed so mature. She was a freshman, and, technically, Michael was, too.

Honestly, when Kristina was around, Michael lit up. His whole being was incandescent. That was a huge relief.

We could count on Michael; he shone, as well, in a crisis.

Our area was stricken with flooding, and our county was suddenly in a state of emergency. Not only that, but Nikki was in labor with her second child. Her basement was flooding, and that's where the furnace, washer, dryer, and family freezer were located. My parents' fish store where I worked was also taking on water. People traveled in boats and kayaks, navigating neighbors to higher ground. We were grateful that our house sat high on a steep hill. The Red Cross trucks delivered lunches and water along with cleaning supplies.

Hearing about the crisis, Michael and Kristina drove in from Buffalo. Between the hot temperatures and no electricity, we were desperately trying to save the tropical fish in the store. Remarkably, we were able to save many of them despite overwhelming odds. Michael took charge of the cleanup and worked nonstop. We kept filling the dumpster outside the store. Everything was wet and extremely heavy, and by the end of the day, it was all I could do to lift items up and heave them into the trash. Both Michael and my (then) son-in-law worked so hard. I could not have managed without them.

Then a string of incidents occurred in Michael's life and looking back, I suppose that's when small cracks really appeared on the surface of his otherwise happy, in-charge demeanor.

Michael had his share of unpleasant events during his stint at Buffalo. One winter evening, someone broke his windshield and stole the radio out of his Jeep. The windshield was far more expensive than what the stereo was worth. He decided to leave the Jeep unlocked after that incident. A week or so later, it happened again: his windshield was broken, even though the Jeep wasn't even locked. It was wintertime in Buffalo, New York. It had to be fixed.

I noticed how much this incident troubled him. He handled it, but the mood it triggered never left completely. It was as if he felt under attack again.

When Michael and Kristina moved into their first apartment complex, Michael's landlord, who was former law enforcement, expressed concerns with the alley along one side of their building. They were on the first floor, but it wasn't flush to the ground—there were steps. Sure enough, shortly after they moved in, Kristina was home alone when an intruder started climbing through the window. Kristina startled him, and he ran off. After the Jeep incidents, I'm sure they worried about a repeat intruder. I know I did.

Again, the threat left its mark on my son. Still, he kept himself moving at an intense pace.

Michael went on to graduate from the University of Buffalo *suma cum laude* with a degree in architecture in May 2010. Kristina also graduated with a degree in physical therapy. Michael's professors predicted a bright future for him. Of course, it was no surprise to us, but always lovely to hear. He was about to enter the University of Kentucky in Lexington. It wasn't his first choice, but he was offered a Teaching Assistant position there. At the time, their architecture program was restructuring. Someone indicated that recommendations hadn't been sent in time for Michael's first choice, Ohio State, so he would attend Kentucky University in Lexington. In the back of my mind, I wondered if he chose Kentucky to be closer to his biological father. Their relationship usually involved fun outings such as kayaking and climbing. Johnson City's high school mascot is a Wildcat, and Michael would once again be a Wildcat. He started to take an interest in Kentucky's outstanding basketball program.

All in all, even with the lingering shadows, it seemed as if the past lay behind and a great future lay ahead. He rarely spoke about Iraq or his military experience. Whereas some combat veterans are free and open with accounts of their life at war, Michael was silent.

Given what was to come, I wish I had pressed him to deal with any lingering issues created by his combat experience.

As it was, we all enjoyed watching him with Kristina – smiling, happy – and none of us suspected the inner scars he was carrying.

CHAPTER 5

GOING ON WITH LIFE – OR TRYING TO

Michael was living in Lexington, Kentucky, eager and excited to begin his master's program. His father helped with the initial move, but after that, he was pretty much on his own. Kristina followed him to Lexington a few months later. Michael settled in with his TA position while undertaking graduate studies. He immersed himself into a barrage of projects, making some influential acquaintances along the way. He had an opportunity to travel to New York City to assist in designing an outdoor living space for an upscale high rise. That was followed by another project involving a documentary that eventually aired on a local TV station. Michael was invited to participate in this project/documentary. After I watched it, I realized that his military background was essential to the development of the project, in addition to his talents as an architect. The tone of the documentary displayed sincere gratitude for first responders and our military. This project entailed making a design involving a beam from the collapsed twin towers of 9/11.

When I watch the documentary today, it's obvious that Michael was still suffering from the effects of war. In the documentary, he stated, "When I laid eyes on the beam, I didn't feel comfortable touching it, let alone cutting it," and he referred to the beam as a sacred piece. But in the end, he decided that the story behind the beam was important, and he was proud of their work. This artistic display would continually travel, representing the loss and devastation that occurred on 9/11. Of course, he knew about that firsthand; he was well aware of the catastrophic loss of life that resulted from 9/11.

As usual, some misfortunes followed. Michael ended up moving several times in a brief period. The first move came early on; his place was small, and Kristina hadn't relocated immediately. It wasn't an ideal situation, and moving's never cheap. Once Kristina joined him, he decided the neighborhood wasn't safe and moved again. The weekend of the move, his father asked him to dog sit for the weekend because he was going out of town. Michael wasn't pleased. He had a busy weekend with his move, but he'd never say no! Sure enough, his father's dog broke out of the fenced-in yard and, of course, Michael had the responsibility to find him. On top of that, he needed to mend the fence. It seemed like Michael couldn't catch a break and that if things could go wrong, they would.

Or maybe it was something I picked up – that, despite all the activity and smiles, he had some kind of dark cloud about him. You could catch a glimpse of it now and again, but I – all of us – were only too happy to have him home safe from combat and going on with his life.

I see now that just pushing behind a past that included violence, bloodshed, and death is a mistake. Air traffic controllers, when they witnessed on their control screens a near miss between two jetliners, are made to take time off for psychological evaluation. Ditto, police officers who discharge their weapons in the line of duty.

Instead, we ignore our combat veteran's past, let pressures mount unchecked, telling ourselves these are just little, everyday things everyone has to deal with – not realizing they can be proverbial straws building up on the camel's back.

Every time Michael moved, he had to move kayaks and a seemingly endless tool supply, not to mention a ninety-gallon aquarium that housed his brackish fish, making a move all that more challenging. By now, they'd adopted Sammy, a rescue Plot-Hound. Sammy was a howler when left alone. Michael and Kristina seemed to like their second home, but I'm pretty confident somebody in that building worked a second or third shift. The move heightened Sammy's anxiety, which added to their stress level, and they worried about their neighbors complaining about Sammy's anxious howling. Michael had additional concerns. It was dark and secluded where Kristina got in and out of her vehicle, especially in the winter when it got dark early. He was adamant about Kristina's safety.

At this point, they decided to move again. This time they explored property options carefully, assuming this would be their final move. It was their third move in less than two years. They finally found a beautiful place close to the university. It seemed perfect! Soon after they moved into the house, they were stunned to find out it was for sale. The sign went up in the front yard shortly after they settled in. Michael was a bit troubled, and he felt somewhat deceived. I'm sure Kristina felt the same. They had no idea what would happen. They didn't have a lease, and that didn't matter anyway because once the property changed hands, a lease would no longer be valid. He suspected another move would be in his future. The realtor had the perfect solution: buy the house! At that point, Michael was confident he wanted out of Kentucky once and for all.

The moves were stressful enough, but then Michael had an unfortunate car accident that ultimately totaled his Jeep Cherokee Limited Edition. My husband had given the Jeep to him while he was in Buffalo. It was in great shape and worth some money prior. Michael didn't carry collision because he was trying to save money. As it turned out, Michael was picking up items as a favor at the time of the accident. The accident definitely could have been worse; at least he wasn't injured. Unfortunately, the vehicle was totaled. He wanted to fix it, but the frame had far too much damage.

Michael seemed to fray a little more each time something like this occurred. The agitation seemed to be more. The time before he could let an incident go seemed longer. His buoyant ability to bound back was quickly diminishing.

I wish I could have helped him more. If I had covered the collision, he would have had the money to get a newer car. I wasn't even aware he had no collision insurance; I guess I did the best I could at the time. I'd recently relocated to Southwest Florida and started a new job with a substantial pay cut.

At the time, Kristina was working in physical therapy and had a long commute. She'd recently purchased a Prius at a Toyota dealership affiliated with her job. That freed up the aging Honda she'd been driving. It had been her late grandmother's car. Her parents had given it to her. Michael took over the Honda and gave Kristina the down payment for the Prius in the amount it was worth if traded. At least that solved his problem of not having a vehicle.

During this time period, Michael expressed little things that stand out in my mind now. He vented a little about the atmosphere in the architectural program. He struggled to buy materials he needed for models and different projects. He wasn't complaining but more or less expressing that colleagues and students viewed things differently. I think he felt a little bit out of touch within this community. It may have been a sign of depression, or maybe he was completely right. He was accustomed to working hard for everything, including the supplies he needed for models.

Not everything was horrible. Michael was doing well in the graduate program, carrying a 4.0 in all but one semester, and even then, he carried a high GPA. He liked his professors and managed to form some new friendships along the way.

Michael was about mid-way through the master's program when Kristina decided physical therapy just wasn't her cup of tea. She enrolled in a mathematical economic course at the University. It looked like they would be staying in Kentucky just a bit longer than they originally planned.

Meanwhile, we were about to welcome Lauren into our family. Steve and Lauren married in late August 2011. The wedding was in Emerald Isle, North Carolina. This fantasy wedding surrounded us with beautiful, aquatic views. The wedding and reception took place at the aquarium. Lauren's parents prepared an exceptional wedding reception. It was hands down the most remarkable and astonishing wedding I've ever attended! The stunning marine views won every guest over. Lauren made a beautiful bride, and she was a lovely addition to our family. I remember Michael's toast that evening, not from the bridal party table, but softly spoken from the side of the dance floor. He said, "Steve is my little brother. Throughout our lives, we'd have a competition going on. I'd golf in eighth grade, and Steve did it in seventh, only he was a way better golfer! I'd go to the state meet in two sports—so did he! I broke school records in multiple sports—so did Steve! I graduated with the most varsity letters setting a school record—he graduated with the same honor, earning more! So here we go again. Cheers to Steve and Lauren! Steve has now beat me to the wedding altar!" Trust me, Michael wasn't bragging; his face was red as he stumbled for the words. Steve had done it again – one-upped Michael by beating him to the altar.

Duane, Laura, Steve, Lauren, Nichole & Michael

If Kristina ever had concerns about Michael early in their relationship, I didn't know about them. Maybe I was the only one who could see he was avoiding negative emotions. Maybe I was the only one who excused his occasional gray moods as the result of all the pressure. I definitely chalked up his tendency to drive himself and overwork as normal. How could I have known then that he had learned to drive himself to exhaustion and beyond while in the service? Like so many service men and women, he just seemed like "the strong, silent type."

The morning after the wedding, all eyes and ears were focused on the weather forecast. A storm was brewing. We were concerned because Steven and Lauren were about to fly to Puerto Rico for their honeymoon cruise. Hurricane Irene was coming, and the storm was heading right toward Lauren's parents' house in North Carolina.

Instead, as usual, the storm changed paths. Let's just say there was never a shortage of storms in our lives. Now Broome County, New York, was in a state of emergency. The hurricane's heavy rain caused flooding, and the damage was catastrophic. The first flood was awful, but this one was much worse—sheer devastation! The neighborhood I'd grown up in, once vibrant and beautiful, was now devastated. The water level rose much higher than the first flood; families still hadn't fully recovered from that one. I'd just returned from North Carolina to Florida and was back at work but purchased a last-minute ticket to head to New York and help. As usual, the timing was terrible, and money was tight. Fortunately, Steve and Lauren's cruise sailed a different route from the one in the hurricane's path, so it didn't disrupt their honeymoon. As for Lauren's parents, they fared better than mine in upstate New York. When I arrived, it was *déjà vu*. The Red Cross was roaming the streets again, and garbage was piled high.

Michael's graduate program and his TA duties resumed. He didn't have time or money to travel to New York. He and Kristina had just returned to Kentucky from the wedding. I didn't want

Michael to go to New York, and my parents discouraged him from coming. True to his loyalty and selflessness, he couldn't or wouldn't sit back without lending a hand.

Both Michael and Kristina traveled to New York to help out. Michael drove all night, with no sleep, and when he arrived, he went at it—full steam ahead, nonstop! With no time to waste, he managed to crank out about a week's worth of work in two days. Just like the first flood, I'm not sure what we would've done without them. Michael's calm presence was such a comfort to my parents. My dad didn't want to get rid of anything. They'd already lost so much from the first flood. Michael was the voice of reason, and my Dad listened to his advice. It's funny how the tables turn with age. My parents were grateful. Michael carried our family through another crisis. I remember the tears in my mother's and father's eyes as they kept thanking Michael. My Dad kept repeating, "Michael, what would we have done without you?!" Michael drove back the same way he'd driven up—another all-nighter with no sleep, only to play catch-up when he returned to the university. His work ethic was second to none; his heart was made of gold! As usual, there was never a dull moment – and more importantly, never a time when Michael seemed able to slow down and stop pushing himself.

We should have asked ourselves why – why was he always pushing himself? And was he running from something?

We were hoping for sunnier days. It was September 2011. Spring was around the corner, and with it would come Michael's master's degree.

And more challenges mounting up. And more driven-ness.

CHAPTER 6

ENGAGED – AND DISENGAGED

Excited and bursting with pride, I could hardly wait for Michael's graduation ceremony. Unlike his high school graduation, after which the Marine recruiter tore the diploma from his hands, Michael was on his way to a life of creativity and fulfillment.

All the fear and worries were behind us for sure. That's what I told myself.

I had purchased our airline tickets well in advance. I didn't realize until boarding the plane that it was Kentucky Derby weekend. Someone must have mentioned it, but I guess it never resonated with me. Until that weekend, I'd never comprehended the magnitude of the Kentucky Derby. The flight was filled with women wearing huge, outlandishly elegant hats for a fun day.

We landed in Louisville, home of the Derby. The airport's theme screamed horse racing; monuments of stallions seemed to be everywhere. Michael wanted to go to the Derby, but getting tickets was a hassle, and it was expensive. Luckily, he'd made other plans, and that turned out to be the next best thing.

After receiving his bachelor's degree from Buffalo, Pete, his virtual twin (they shared a birthday) and close friend, had advised him, "Mike, get your graduate degree immediately following your bachelor's because once bills start piling, you'll never go back to a higher education." Michael took Pete's advice, and now we were sitting in the audience, watching his graduation ceremony. During the commencement, the speaker invited any military member past, present, or future to stand and be recognized.

Michael did not stand.

I was confused and a bit stunned. Michael's father confronted him as soon as we left the building; he asked why he didn't rise and accept the honor. Michael shrugged his shoulders and never answered.

Maybe he just didn't want others to know he served and would rather not talk about his experiences.

Later, I would realize it was a big sign of something happening deep beneath the bright, happy face Michael normally showed to the world. I didn't put it together with the occasional dark moods and his being uncomfortable with nightfall.

His father and stepmother invited us for a dinner celebration they were hosting at their place after the graduation ceremony. As usual, his paternal grandparents were present. It was a pleasant, friendly gathering.

I would later realize, too, that Michael probably had few adult males in his life who he could turn to if he needed to discuss anything that might be troubling him. And given the fact that he was truly a "can-do" kind of young man, he probably would have tried to solve any issues he had totally on his own.

At the dinner, my mind drifted to the first time I met Kristina's mother, Barb, in Buffalo, when Michael and Kristina graduated a day apart. We had a nice dinner out, a small, informal get-together. Michael's father, stepmother, and paternal grandparents were there that day, too. I'll never forget that

Buffalo graduation. It was unseasonably cold for May, brutal for those of us coming from Florida.

Kristina looked beautiful. She wore a lovely green dress, and when she had opened the door to leave for the commencement, Michael stopped dead in his tracks. His smile was so bright it instantly warmed the atmosphere and melted our hearts. I'll never forget the look on his face: *lovestruck*. He was beaming, and she was radiant! For a split second, it was as though nobody else was in the room but the two of them. My mother and I witnessed this delight, this testimony of love. Michael pulled out chairs and opened doors for Kristina, treating her like royalty. She appreciated the treatment, and it was so obvious that she adored him.

I'd been looking forward to meeting Kristina's parents, and both my mother and I instantly connected with her mother, Barb. Our conversation flowed smoothly, as though we'd known each other for years. It was hard to believe it was our first encounter. I could tell Barb, like Kristina, was a kind soul. The apple hadn't fallen far from the tree. We shared things we had in common, such as family names, as well as experiences her mother and I had growing up with our siblings. It didn't take long for me to know that Kristina was the one for Michael, and I was extremely happy for them.

But in that moment, it was about his graduate degree. All in all, the event capped off a long journey. Michael's father and stepmother had prepared a lovely celebration dinner. The food was delicious, and the conversation was friendly.

If I was looking for signs that Michael was okay, they were there. And I was looking for them, because, as his mother, that's what I wanted to see.

The next day was the Derby, a big deal in Kentucky. Michael had planned for us to spend the day at Keene Downs, a racetrack right down the road from his and Kristina's place. It felt like the real deal. Not that I've ever attended the Kentucky Derby, but the magnitude and ambiance were like no other racetrack I'd ever experienced. A gigantic screen sat right in the middle of the track, similar to those in old drive-in movies, only this one was bigger and sharper and was playing the live lead-up to the race. The betting lines at the track were exceptionally long, and every few feet were bars with lines three or more people deep. I was finally going to try a mint julep.

We all celebrated. Michael and Kristina had a beer, maybe two—it was extremely hot. Michael was driving, so he did not overindulge. He was always a responsible driver. They seemed so happy that weekend, smiling and laughing, their future bright and spreading out ahead. Kristina made sure Michael was wearing sunscreen because of his pale complexion. That wasn't the first time I'd seen her make sure he wore sunscreen. As long as Kristina was around, Michael wasn't getting sunburned. He may have catered to her, but she definitely looked out for him, too.

I was taken by the sweetness between them, and my heart was full. Again, his over-responsibility was in play, though – his insistence on taking care of us all.

Many in the crowd were dressed up, the men in suits, the women in beautiful dresses, and those fancy hats. We bet on a horse named Michael and won a little bit of money – nothing colossal, just enough to keep us gambling. Surely, this was a sign. "Michael" was our lucky horse, and our Michael was living under a lucky star now, with a smart, lovely companion at his side.

As for the mint julep, thank goodness we only bought one. None of us could drink it. It was potent—the strongest drink I've ever tried, and I'm pretty sure it's a drink you have to acquire a taste for. We all tried it and chuckled as we tried to pass it off on each other. We did a lot of laughing and smiling that weekend. It would be a wonderful memory.

Beyond the graduation fun, there were other signs that things were going Michael's way. He was about to put his talents to good and gainful use.

His former boss from Buffalo, NY, contacted him about designing and building his daughter's dream home. Michael was incredibly flattered. I'm sure they planned on Mike being a hands-on worker. As this was a *future* dream house, however, it wasn't happening in a day, or even a few weeks. They were just preparing to buy land. Michael drove to New York to see the property and was pleasantly surprised; it was a prime piece of property with breathtaking views of the steep valleys and crystal blue waters of the Finger Lakes. It was a project he was excited about and looking forward to.

In the meantime, Michael needed a plan for his immediate future, the kind that involved a paycheck at the end of a week. He buckled down and composed a lengthy resume. Since Kristina was now enrolled in a Mathematical Economics course at the university, they would continue living in Lexington until she graduated.

If there were a few more small signs of hidden issues – an unexplainable, down day here or there – they quickly vanished in a string of good-news events.

Fortunately, Michael was hired immediately by a local architectural firm. He was also offered a part-time teaching position at the University of Kentucky in the architectural department. Michael gladly accepted both offers, and this allowed them to stay in Kentucky while Kristina finished up her education. It was nice to see him finally reap the benefits of all his hard work. It seemed like he had moved on, leaving the war behind; things were starting to fall into place. I was happy as I watched him blossom! He took his position at the University and the care of his students very seriously; they were a priority, he liked to challenge his students.

I knew Michael would be awesome at teaching. After all, he had taught me far more than I had ever taught him. His lens captured observations most others missed. He noticed everything around him and saw the whole picture, never focusing totally on the focal point. He thought outside the box and had views beyond my scope.

Maybe Michael's tendency to take on too much was a signal. But given his creative mind and vast energies, that seemed normal – if not a little worrisome to me as his mother.

A coworker at the architectural firm had a fiancé who owned and operated a food truck, and his business was booming. He decided to open a permanent place and needed some design work. As if Michael's other responsibilities were not enough, he took on the project. Michael was a hard worker, and once he took on a project, he worked on it until it was complete. He ended up doing an enormous amount of work for this start-up restaurant, but he enjoyed it. Not necessarily the grunt work, but he was able to employ his creative skills. He even handmade some of the furniture; his work was extraordinarily detailed, with massive amounts of woodwork. This little restaurant/grill was going to serve Greek cuisine. Part of Michael's challenge was being the jack of all trades. In the end, I'd describe the atmosphere as "modern but quaint," if that is at all possible. He did a bit of everything, even rewiring the whole place. When the final electrical inspection took place, the inspector asked if he needed a job. Apparently, his rewiring work was excellent.

I'd be lying if I said I wasn't concerned about all the work Michael continued to take on. At times, he was exhausted. It was clear he strove to go above and beyond anyone's expectations. For instance, as the restaurant work was being done, they insisted on giving him his meals for free. He told me that the food was delicious but that he felt bad they wouldn't charge him, and in the end, told them he wouldn't eat there anymore unless they let him pay.

Meanwhile, Michael and Kristina still had the burden of dealing with their living arrangements. The house they were renting was still for sale, and realtors were rushing in and out regularly. Michael and Kristina were well aware that they needed to stay at least another year for Kristina to complete her Mathematical Economics course, so they started the dreaded hunt for yet another apartment, which was very difficult in a college town. Michael wasn't looking forward to another move; just the thought of uprooting and hefting around all their belongings again bothered him, and he felt deceived because when he and Kristina had rented the place, the real estate transaction was deliberately left out. Obviously, moving again wasn't in the plan. Little things were creeping up, and tension was starting to build.

I wished I could have helped him, but I was too far away to help much. Michael always made an effort to help others, but he didn't ask others for help. I suppose that after having assistance with their first few moves, they were probably too embarrassed to ask.

I began to wonder about the strain Michael was putting on himself. Besides his other jobs, he was a mentor and volunteered in a reading program, and he'd been working with a young foster boy. The assignment they had included bringing items from home, little things that reflected the story and themselves. Since his foster parents wouldn't allow items to leave the house, Michael took it upon himself to buy related trinkets each week. He wanted this experience to be a positive one. Somehow, he managed to find time, despite the fact he had no free time. He worked nonstop yet still managed to do charitable acts. He thought it was essential to give back.

My concerns were soon set aside when a bright, wonderful event happened.

It was almost Christmas when Michael made an important call to Kristina's parents. He'd been stewing about this for quite some time; he thought the proper thing would be to fly to New York to talk to them in person. I agreed, but unfortunately, it wasn't practical, and I assured him Kristina's parents would understand. Eventually, he gathered up the courage to call and ask for their blessing.

Michael's plan was to take Kristina to the same place they went on their very first date in Buffalo, and he did. On their date, Michael popped the question. Kristina said yes! It's a good thing since he had already planned a celebration. He'd called several close friends in Buffalo, pre-arranging for them to meet after the proposal to join the celebration. When he called with the news, I was elated. I felt my concern for Michael's wellbeing lessen. Maybe he'd stop driving himself so hard and enjoy life a little more! And besides this upcoming wedding, we now had another graduation—Kristina's—to look forward to in the spring.

Michael & Kristina

Yes, things were definitely looking up.

A few days later, I was ready to celebrate a co-worker's birthday on New Year's Eve when I received a very pleasant and welcomed phone call. Michael wanted to let me know that they'd just found the perfect place to have their wedding reception. He was extremely excited about an old refurbished barn they'd found for the event, one with a unique architectural charm. "Rustic, but extraordinarily elegant," he said. "We both love it."

I have to admit it wasn't what I envisioned for their wedding reception, but they were so excited and happy and, of course, it was their wedding to plan. I was pleasantly surprised when I viewed the venue online. I saw that it was a spectacular barn. Michael sounded elated; he and Kristina were so impressed with the barn's unique design. They had also decided on a date. The wedding would be July 4, 2015.

When Michael hung up, I felt elated, too. It looked like a very happy new year was coming our way.

And so, on the surface, Michael continued to seem happy. The occasional dips into a gray mood could be overlooked – though I wished he would have talked to me or his stepdad or anyone about them.

I had no idea that, with his tendency to go deep, his kindness and love for people were working against him. Was it painful images of the helicopter crash – for which he held himself responsible – that were coming back to torture him? Was he being re-traumatized by dark visions of what he'd seen in war?

I would ask myself over and over. Shouldn't I have known that beneath his good cheer and bravado, a sensitive, overly responsible person was in pain?

I know now it is a characteristic of those who love combat veterans. We so badly want our loved one to be well, to forget the past and move on, that we can overlook a lot.

CHAPTER 7

SILENT CRIES FOR HELP

A ll the signs were good. How could any of us have known what lay just ahead?

Michael and Kristina set aside time to visit for Thanksgiving; they'd drive from Kentucky all the way to Southwest Florida. No surprise, they'd be stuck in a traffic jam along the way. Heading through Orlando around Thanksgiving is brutal–traffic's heavy. Steve and Lauren arrived from Jacksonville a day or two later. It was nice to have a portion of our family gathered for Thanksgiving.

Michael was the trooper who cooked the turkey; he'd placed it in a pit he'd dug in the backyard, then smoked it with a hickory stick. I'll admit I'm glad Michael cooked the dinner. I'm not the cook in our house; my husband is the chef. My mother usually handled special occasions. Duane doesn't care for turkey. He ate far too much while on dialysis, it's just a lousy taste memory. If it were up to him, we'd be eating tenderloins.

As usual, everything seemed right on the surface.

We ventured out to Fort Myers and Sanibel Beaches. On Thanksgiving morning, we'd go to the manatee park nearby. Michael, Kristina, Steve, and Lauren took a trip to Orlando, where they visited The Harry Potter theme park, utterly enjoying their experience. A swamp boat tour in the Everglades was next. Duane tagged along for that; I opted out. I'd stay home and take care of the dogs since we had five that weekend. Four Mastiffs and poor Sammy. Besides, whenever I thought about the Everglades, I thought of giant snakes. Snakes are my biggest fear. For some reason, I'm not afraid of spiders. Michael often said, "Mom, you should fear spiders more. At least with snakes, you see them coming."

It's a treasured family gathering. As I said, everything seemed about right.

But not *quite*. Small clouds were appearing on the horizon.

Once sun started setting Michael, starting turning all the lights on. He said, "It's dark in here. It's depressing."

I was perplexed. Our great room had windows that were six feet tall, with a small break, topped off with additional four to five feet of glass up to the ceiling. There was plenty of light and a lovely evening afterglow even as the sun went down.

Also, I'd never ever heard him use the word "depressing."

Even with the beautiful pinks and golds reflected in by the evening sky, the peaceful atmosphere the rest of us basked in seemed far from wherever Michael's mind and soul were.

Spring 2014 was just around the corner, and Michael's 32nd birthday was coming up in March.

Well aware of student debt, I'd send him a check as part of his birthday present to cover the remaining balance on a smaller student loan. It was a mere grand, but I knew any little bit would help. Not that I usually spent a thousand dollars on birthday gifts. I certainly wasn't making enough money to give lavish gifts. I realized any aid in reducing his student debt would be one less bill. If I did it here and there, we'd chip away at his debt together.

Michael was very grateful. There were plenty of other student loans, not outlandish for an architect with a Master's degree, but money owed.

Michael couldn't have possibly worked any harder. He'd been working far too many hours with absolutely no personal time.

In hindsight, this might have been a warning. Was he only trying to retire his debt? Or was he avoiding something?

I noticed a disparaging attitude starting to creep in.

Michael was contemplating a trip to Mexico because a good friend was getting married. The wedding was in May. Andy was his friend from childhood. He'd faced the dilemma–attend or decline? Michael wanted to participate; unfortunately, time and funds were sparse. On top of that, they were still dreading another move. Plenty was happening. Michael opted in; he'd go to Mexico. He and Kristina were finally able to have a relaxing mini vacation. They ended up staying at a different location than everyone else. Michael indicated he somehow managed to screw that up. He was very critical and derogatory about himself. There was a hint of "I never get it right." In the aftermath, his friends suggested the separate location was deliberate. Either way, it just didn't sound like Michael.

Soon, I noticed that he'd gone from happy-go-lucky, the glass is half full, to the complete opposite. He was mocking himself as a loser.

Maybe he was just tired and overwhelmed, and this was just a signal that he really needed the vacation.

After returning from Mexico, his attitude changed back to upbeat and relaxed. The opportunity to spend time with Kristina and his good friends had been a rare getaway, and, to my great relief, he sounded refreshed. Much better.

Unfortunately, it wasn't too long before he started sounding critical again. He began talking about a military, ten-year reunion – ten years!

I realized that he rarely mentioned the military anymore. It was a subject he never brought up, not with me anyway. As for the reunion, he sounded eager to attend. It would involve travel, and he would need to save money. Not a big deal since it was still about a year away.

Michael was still working at the architectural firm and the college, locked into at least another semester, while Kristina finished up her Mathematical Economics degree. She and Michael had a low-key celebration with a nice dinner out. Kristina insisted her parents not travel. She wasn't planning to attend the graduation ceremony. Kristina undertook a series of expensive math exams for certification, which she passed. Michael was so impressed with her and often bragged how bright she was. You could tell by the way he looked at her just how much in love with her he was.

That made my heart soar.

By late summer, Kristina was looking for a job; they were planning to leave Kentucky. There was no dire rush, as Michael was committed to the university until the new year, but he insisted he could find work anywhere. He felt Kristina should find the job she wanted, and he'd follow wherever that might be.

At the same time, there was a wedding to plan – a long-distance one for all of us, with the exception of Kristina's parents. That began to occupy my mind. A wedding, a young couple together forever... the hope of children for them and more grandchildren for me.

Kristina's friend had a shower scheduled in early September, prompting her to plan a trip home around this event. She decided to drive to New York State and, after the shower, start tackling some wedding arrangements before having to settle into a new job. It made sense; once she had a new job, she wouldn't have time. Very sensible.

As usual, Michael called every day, though many days, the conversations were rushed because he'd be in a hurry. Though one conversation would stand out in my mind later.

Robin Williams just died. I felt horrible; his suicide was sad. Robin made everyone laugh with his jokes and his jovial demeanor. Such talent. So successful. I was a real fan and just loved him.

I said, "I don't get it. Someone like Robin Williams could afford to get help. He could easily have gotten the best care available."

Michael said, "Mom, you don't understand. It's not about that."

"What do you mean?" It sounded like Michael was condoning his actions.

We talked about suicide at great length in this particular conversation.

"What about his family?" I insisted. "What about his daughter?"

"Mom, it's not about them. You don't get it."

"If he sought professional help, he'd be alive today."

Michael wasn't agreeing and kept repeating. "You really don't get it."

What on earth was he saying?

To me, as a Catholic, suicide was just not acceptable.

But more troublesome, Michael was saying things that were entirely out of character.

After I took into account the hours he was working, the lack of sleep, I chalked it up to that.

Now I know that conversation was a warning sign. To this day, I can't believe I missed the opportunity to flat-out ask him about his state of mind. Why didn't I ask if he was thinking about taking his life?

In the coming weeks, we had several conversations that seemed normal and reasonable. Still, there were more and more conversations in which Michael sounded out-of-kilter. Michael shared some happy news about things in general; unfortunately, this wasn't very often. Again, I chalked it up to his work situation.

He had just completed a project for his firm, which they'd used to bid on a big job. It was his vision and model that earned his company the contract they'd just won. He had worked extremely hard on this particular project, going above and beyond – in fact, when they landed the contract, it was announced at the firm when he wasn't even present. Nobody included him, minimizing his contribution.

In more than one conversation, I could tell it bothered him. I think it hurt, more than anything, that everyone was celebrating the good news but him, when it was his "win," his hard work.

As summer ended and pre-season fall sports began, Michael started talking about football. Almost obsessively. He would suddenly blurt out that the sport should be banned. I found it very odd since, as a youngster, he played peewee football and loved it.

He felt the sport led to severe head injuries and insisted he wasn't happy with the NFL regarding traumatic brain injuries. Suddenly, he'd start unpacking thoughts about growing up, saying way too much time was wasted in the gym.

Wow, I thought, *I wish he'd told me then*. Then I kidded him about his time on the boys' gymnastics team, which I really couldn't afford at the time. I reminded him that he had begged me.

There was more grumbling about sports – expressions that were entirely out of character.

With each passing week, he continued to become more derogatory.

I wished he could get a break; find time to rest.

Meanwhile, there were other distractions. I'd be traveling to New York, where I had a court hearing regarding grandparents' visitation rights. Nikki shared custody with her ex-husband then, making it impossible for the boys to visit us in Florida.

Kristina's friend's shower was approaching; she'd be traveling to New York to secure a church. The down payment on the hall was already secured, but there was plenty of other arrangements to make, like finding a dress, locating a caterer, a photographer, a floral arranger…

I focused my mind on happy thoughts of the beautiful day ahead for all of us.

Michael continued working ungodly hours, staying up many nights. Once, he said one of his students was upset about having to work all night and complaining about the hours - right before he was about to head to bed.

Michael told him, "Well, I have just enough time to go home, take a shower, and get to work."

Clearly, the overnight work was draining his energy physically and mentally. Some nights he got no rest at all; he desperately needed to recuperate. He did many overnight shifts in the military and he did them during the flood.

I knew Michael was wearing down. Sleep is a basic necessity and the sleep deprivation was taking its toll.

When we spoke, his tone was increasingly cynical, pessimistic even about little things – to my surprise, even with the wedding. He said he didn't care to ask anyone to stand up for him; weddings were too expensive; he didn't want to inconvenience anyone. He'd have Steve stand up for him, and Kristina would have her sister.

I assured him we all saw it as a joyful celebration. Our family and his friends would be there for him and Kristina on their special day.

I said, "Michael, if you're asked to be in a wedding, it's an honor and a privilege. Not some kind of thankless, unpleasant duty."

What was going on in his mind?

He continued to see the dark side of things more and more each day. Fewer of his friends, he said, lived in New York. "Who's going to want to come all the way back there just to stand up in a wedding?"

In September, Kristina was set to leave for New York. To her surprise, and probably some dismay, Michael said he would prefer she stay home.

She couldn't, of course.

All the arrangements for the shower were in place, and she would be able to spend some relaxing and fun time with friends and family. Also, she would be taking care of more wedding arrangements.

Off she went, arriving in upstate New York to prep for their big day.

On September 11, 2014, Michael called to inform me Kristina made it to New York State safely.

I noticed the minute I heard his voice, however, that he wasn't doing well. He sounded extremely dispirited.

My mind was on the terrible news, and his – I imagined – was, too.

Every TV channel and radio station blasted constant reminders of the devastation that occurred that morning in Manhattan, where two hijacked jetliners had crashed into the World Trade Center's twin towers, another had crashed into the Pentagon, and a fourth had nose-dived into a field in Pennsylvania. The footage played over and over again. It was incredibly depressing.

But the national disaster was not the only thing on Michael's mind.

Sounding disheartened, he said, "Mom, I've made some serious mistakes in my life."

"Michael," I said, alarmed, "Are you okay? Is everything okay with you and Kristina?"

"Yeah, Mom, everything is okay with Kristina. It's not that. She's great."

"Then what do you mean?"

He quickly shut down and didn't share more.

What are the serious mistakes? I pondered. *What is he talking about? Why won't he tell me?*

I said, "If you're not happy where you are and with what you're doing, move on. Start over fresh somewhere else."

I knew he really wanted to leave Kentucky. "Is it the thought of having to move yet again?"

"No."

"Is it work?"

"No."

I groped around in my mind. He was working multiple job sites, pulled in every direction, over-worked, unquestionably suffering from sleep deprivation.

I almost said, "You don't sound right," but didn't. Maybe it was just exhaustion speaking.

I reminded him that everyone who worked with him praised his work ethic; they all had great things to say. I also reminded him about all that he and we had to look forward to, especially the wedding.

I said, "I have a chunk of money saved for the wedding celebration. You can use that."

The conversation on 9/11 was significant. Again, I've had a perpetual regret that I didn't flat out ask him if he had thoughts about harming himself–that I didn't hop on a flight to see him. I had no idea what physical condition he was in, what he looked like, what was going through his mind.

I often wonder if I'd had a smartphone, could it have made a difference? If I texted then, could I have reread some of the comments and realized what was happening? Or we could have face-timed, and then I could have seen his sad state. Michael's demeanor would've been obvious; if I'd seen him, I would have known.

If I'm honest, I have to admit I always considered Michael our family rock – our Marine, the strong, sensible one. I assumed he'd be fine after 9/11's terrible shockwaves passed.

Now all the missed opportunities are apparent; it just makes forgiving myself that much harder. The signs were right there. Hindsight is 20/20. As for me, I was completely blind.

I did ask Michael before we hung up, "Are you sure you're going to be okay?"

"Yes," he said quietly. "I'll be just fine."

A few days later, Sunday, I spent time at the beach in the morning with my husband, and, later in the day, I had a glass of wine in my hand when Michael called again.

Kristina was busy in New York. She and her mother made some plans regarding the wedding. I told Michael the happy news I just heard from my daughter Nikki that his nephew, my grandson Dante, had just run a 5K and proudly informed him that Dante won in his age category.

A runner himself, Michael's voice sounded upbeat, happy. The usual questions came: What was his time? Where was the race?

"That's great," he said, enthused. "Fantastic. Tell him I'm proud."

No, I thought. *I'll tell him myself.*

When I asked about him, the tone had changed since our last conversation. He was doing good; everything was fine. No complaints, no problems. He was going to call Nikki so he could speak to Dante and congratulate him. It felt great. I was glad he had done a complete 180-turn from the conversation a few days before. It had been a long time since I'd heard his voice sound that enthusiastic. And yet.

Why, deep down, did I have the feeling things weren't as good as he was projecting? How those "terrible mistakes" he mentioned cryptically so suddenly righted themselves?

That's the last time I would hear Michael's voice. Life was about to plummet into the darkest depths. I later learned that Michael called everybody, including his brother Steve and my parents. I never saw it coming yet it was right there in plain sight. Every sign, every word, every call; it wasn't like we didn't talk regularly. How did I miss all the signs?

I realize now, my comments, my advice during his challenging time, were precisely, explicitly all the things you should never say. At least, not to someone who is contemplating suicide.

On Monday, September 15, 2014, I was home from work, had already swum my usual laps, and we were getting ready to sit down and eat dinner.

My phone rang. Because he was the one who always called at dinnertime, I answered, "Hi, Michael.

"No, Mom, it's Steve."

"Hey, Steve. What's up?" Steve seldom called. That last time was when he was in the hospital with a collapsed lung. "Is everything okay?"

"No, Mom, what are you doing? Are you driving?"

"No, I'm home."

"Are you sitting down?"

"Steve, what's going on?" He was starting to make me nervous.

Steve was stumbling on his words.

"Something happened to Michael."

I was confused. Michael was in Kentucky; Steve was in Jacksonville. Why was he calling me about Michael?

"What happened?" I felt my throat tightening.

"Mike's gone."

"What do you mean gone?"

"Michael is dead."

I could hear someone screaming; it was me.

"Was it a car accident? What happened?"

Steve did not answer.

"Tell me. *What happened*?"

"Mom, it doesn't matter," he answered, his voice full of pain.

"Michael is gone."

CHAPTER 8

IMMEDIATE AFTERMATH

"Steve-what happened to Michael?"

"Mom, it was suicide. Michael took his own life."

When the answer to my anguished question came, I couldn't grasp it.

This could not be right. It was a big mistake.

No. Oh NO, NO! I started calling Michael – and kept calling his phone, but it went straight to voicemail.

Losing a son was devastating enough; suicide was incomprehensible.

I found myself on my knees, my breathing shallow and panicky, begging, *Please, God, don't let this be true.*

How can you feel numb *and* at the same time feel immense pain? How would I tell my parents?

I called Nichole, and her reaction was like mine – disbelief, hysteria, shrieking. "No, No, *NO!*" I begged her to gather her composure because l needed her to go to my parents' house, so when I called them, we could tell them together. Since my father had severe heart problems, I was anxious the news could trigger a heart attack.

In a thick cloud mentally, I told my family I had no idea who found Michael or where he was – only the terrible news.

My parents and my sister Susan were devastated; it didn't seem real. How was this possible?

Michael had no ongoing history of drinking or drug abuse, no mental illness, or depression.

Check that. Vaguely, my thoughts circled back to those down times. The stresses. The darker comments he let slip now and again. But they were just blips on the screen, not flashing yellow or red lights. What did we not know? What did he not tell us?

How could someone so loved and talented end their life? It didn't make any sense.

Now I know that there can be a huge disconnect between the way someone presents themselves on the surface and how they are really feeling deep inside. I wish I had known that sooner. I wish I had pressed Michael to seek support – any kind of support – when he voiced his negative feelings and quickly discounted them, assuring me he would be "all right."

Finally, I found the strength to call Kristina. She was in total shock, just like the rest of us, and sick to her stomach. A few details came to light.

Michael's boss had concerns when he didn't show up for work and wasn't answering his phone. He'd driven to their apartment complex and found Michael in the garage – already gone.

Listening to her, I understood how she felt – and how his poor boss felt, finding Michael. I'm sure his life changed forever at that moment. Later, he would tell me, "Michael left enormous shoes to fill. I don't think it's possible for anyone to fill his shoes… all the talent he had."

When I hung up from talking to Kristina, I envisioned the scene where Michael was found. It kept playing back in my mind over and over again, haunting me.

Later that evening, I received a call from Michael's father. Even in his terrible upset, he went to great lengths to thank me for raising Michael, complimenting me on what a wonderful gentleman Michael turned out to be, ever so gracious with his words. He asked if Michael had a will.

I balked at this turn to business. "No, why would he? He's only 32."

He skipped over that. His wife worked for a respectable funeral home, and he said Michael's body would be transported there, assuring me they'd take excellent care of him.

His father graciously put together an obituary. Kristina's name appeared near the end. I felt she should be listed as the first survivor; after all, she and Michael shared a life together. After I pointed that out, it was immediately changed. I somehow overlooked an additional error regarding Michael's deployments. Tours in Afghanistan and Iraq were listed. Michael had only deployed to Iraq. This was one of the first blunders; there were plenty to follow.

I was awake all night, my soul in turmoil, trying to absorb this reality. I sat at a table assembling pictures, crying, heartsick. I wanted to make sure I captured essential memories, and since we'd be on the road, I wouldn't be able to carry vast amounts of photo albums. Michael's father created a video and slide shows, and I scanned numerous photos to send him, sobbing with every image I scanned.

Morning came, and I didn't know what to do with myself. Stay home, and bury my face in pillows? Or go to work and lose myself in simple, mindless, routine duties?

Despite feeling distraught and awful, I decided to head into work. Somehow, I cleaned myself up. I had the fish to plan for; I needed to leave instructions for their care. I tried to work. I couldn't. I had to juggle this terrible rollercoaster of realities – one minute floating above it all, the next minute seeing images of Michael in my mind's-eye....

At work, my coworker's reactions indicated the sad news had traveled. Karin, a co-worker and friend, had lost her daughter to suicide years earlier. She was one of the first I approached. I'll never forget the grim look on her face; her lips were quivering and she was trembling as I entered her office. Horrified, she held me tight, and we wept together. I could tell she truly felt my pain. She relived her loss; we shared this torment, this agony.

When the rest of my co-workers started flooding in, before I knew it, we were in a huge group, hugging, sobbing. I resembled a boxer who had just lost a fight; my eyes were swollen nearly shut and my face was puffy from crying. I learned just how fast you can become dehydrated from crying.

Even with the pain, it helped to be in the presence of people who deeply cared and felt our loss.

Today, I say to anyone who is struggling with any kind of pain, let alone the pain of loss, do not keep it to yourself. Pain shared is not less, but it is more easily borne.

Delvia dictated I not stay at work; both she and Yenisey insisted I not drive home. If I was going to drive to Jacksonville in the morning to be with my son Steve and his wife, I'd need something to calm my nerves. They encouraged me to seek medical help; they'd accompany me to the doctor's office.

My doctor prescribed a low dose of anxiety meds. She is also Catholic and graciously vowed to say a rosary for Michael. I couldn't have asked for more. She cautioned me not to over-medicate, saying it was essential that I process what was happening. I took her advice and used the medication sparingly.

We were spread out. What followed was some back-and-forth emails and phone conversations about where to have calling hours. I consulted with Kristina, too, and we reached an agreement. We would honor Michael's express wish to be cremated. This would make our plan feasible – calling hours, first in Kentucky, then in New York – as we would only be transporting his ashes.

His ashes.

Those words numbed me as I tried to plan for what came next. There would be calling hours on Friday evening – *this very next Friday* – for my son. I could hardly breathe. From Kentucky, we'd travel in our rental car to upstate New York. On Sunday evening, we planned calling hours in our small hometown of Johnson City, and a funeral Mass would follow on Monday morning.

We arrived at Steve and Lauren's in Jacksonville on Wednesday. I still hadn't slept; nevertheless, I had arrangements to make. Car rental, return airline tickets, our plans for calling hours, Mass with a luncheon for everyone after.

If only things had gone smoothly from this point on.

When we arrived at the funeral home in Kentucky the afternoon of the viewing, things began to heat up.

A discussion occurred about the casket being open or closed. Kristina had expressed earlier that she was entirely against that idea as she didn't want to see Michael like that. I thought that since she was his fiancé, we should honor her request.

Not everyone agreed, and the subject became intense. In the end, we decided to have a few moments to view Michael before calling hours. Kristina would wait an hour before coming.

At the end of that hour, however, the coffin remained open. Like Kristina, I, too, hadn't decided if I wanted to view Michael like that. I had refrained from going up to the open casket.

We'd been busy setting up photo displays and viewing urns on a separate floor. That hour went fast. I'd met some of Michael's colleagues from the university. One said she would never forget this, and said, "I'll take the time each and every day to make sure those surrounding me are okay." It was clear the shock waves were felt, and a feeling of guilt flowed everywhere. She continued, "Whether it's a thank you, a smile, or a simple 'is everything okay?' I'm going to reach out to other people."

In the end, the coffin remained open. Kristina endured calling hours sitting in the back of the funeral home. I understood why she wouldn't want that image embedded in her head because what I forced myself to see remains as the last vivid image of my handsome son.

He was dressed in his military blues. I held his hand and kissed him goodbye. It was surreal, and I kept thinking, *That's Michael lying in the casket. How is this possible? How could this have been prevented?*

That horrific picture is forever etched in my mind and my soul. Perhaps Kristina's choice was the right one; the way things unfolded, I didn't have an option.

Michael did look peaceful; none of us were.

I became distraught at the funeral home.

I'd been approached right before calling hours to sign papers agreeing to cremate Michael's remains. The cremation was scheduled for early the next morning.

My heart dropped, and I needed to sit, barely able to breathe. The thought of what was going to happen was terrifying.

Michael's father sat next to me and put his arms around me, reiterating that this was the right thing to do. That it's what Michael wanted. He continued with confidence and kindness, saying everything would be taken care of and arrangements to expedite the cremation were already in place. This, he said, would allow ample time for our services in New York.

Again, I had another strange unsettled feeling – very much like when I had felt all but forced to sign the military's parental consent form. It just didn't feel right.

For many long minutes, I was frozen, with everyone approaching me, trying to ease my fears. Everyone, including Michael's father, kept assuring me I was doing the right thing.

After quite some time, I stood up, knees buckling, nearing emotional collapse. I somehow walked into the office to sign. I didn't think I'd be able to because I was shaking so badly.

In my head, I kept saying, *This doesn't feel right.*

But then again, how can signing papers for your child's cremation feel right? Parents aren't supposed to deal with this.

Against my better judgment and my intuition to *not* sign, I signed that consent form.

I calmed myself as best I could, thinking, *Let's get through these calling hours and bring Michael home so he can rest in peace.*

Later, I wish once again that I had paid attention to my inner voice.

That evening, the funeral home was packed, the line extending out the door as hundreds of people poured through – Michael's architect students, college colleagues, co-workers, and even some of Michael's former comrades from his Marine family were there.

The funeral home itself looked amazing. It was a tribute to Michael and everything he enjoyed: kayaks, climbing gear, architectural models from Buffalo and Kentucky University. It was like a museum of his life. Pictures were displayed everywhere, and a fantastic slideshow played throughout the evening. I'd brought Michael's military photo in a large frame, along with a few small photo albums. I also had his prestigious Air medal that he had earned during the Iraq War. Nikki put together a few beautifully designed collages with favorite family memories.

We would go on and hold calling hours at the funeral home in Johnson City, New York, as planned. Hundreds of people were in attendance, viewing Michael's military photo and Air medal.

But no Michael. And not even the urn containing his ashes – which had been promised.

We proceeded with the scheduled funeral Mass, forced now to place an empty box on the altar.

It was raining; everyone stood in the back of the church as the military honor-guard service commenced. "Taps" sounded, reiterating pride and commitment to country. A 21-gun salute began. I felt every shot fired, each one piercing my already broken heart. The flag was folded in front of Kristina and me. Though I wanted to share it with her, she insisted I take it.

Without a doubt, these were the saddest, darkest moments of my life – made worse by my yearning for Michael's missing remains to be present, to be blessed on his way into eternity.

Setting my personal story aside for a moment, I want to offer these thoughts.

My strongest pieces of advice directly following a shocking event such as suicide are these:

Rely on those who are trustworthy, your loved ones.

Don't make important decisions when you're in shock. You're not capable of making good choices then.

When friends and family you know and trust reach out, embrace them and accept their support.

Having said that, don't rely on just anyone; not everyone is virtuous. Follow your heart, never stray from respecting others. Try to put yourself in their shoes.

One of your personal complications may be that of a mental fog setting in, as it did for me. I was physically present but unable to think straight.

In particular, I recall an episode of fog, an example of my state of mind ten months following Michael's death. I'd made a quick run through the grocery store just around the corner from work, picking up dinner. I paid for several items, hopped into my car, and drove my twenty-mile commute home only to realize when I got home, I didn't have one bag. I paid, and I had the receipt – just not the groceries. I was running through the motions, but I wasn't present. No wonder my weight plummeted under a hundred pounds.

You need not push or punish yourself for being in this state; it is part of a tragic loss, as you're trying to readjust to the new and painful reality.

If this state persists month after month and you are unable to deal with necessary activities, such as sleeping, eating, work, and any interactions with other people – I strongly recommend that you seek help from a clergy person, counselor, or therapist. It was after that grocery incident that I realized I needed help. Respect the fact that you are in shock and grieving. Seek help. It's important to find someone you trust, someone with similar faith and views. I found talking to those that have lost children the most beneficial because they understand and get it. Grief is a powerful emotion; compassion and empathy can be every bit as powerful to aid in your healing and ability to eventually move on. Listening to those who had also suffered impacted me in a very positive way. I knew I wasn't alone. Their stories and their recovery gave me hope.

Lastly, it's only natural to want to honor our loved ones and any difficulties they have left us to deal with. No matter what disagreements occur among survivors, honoring must be the focus – the last act of love.

CHAPTER 9

MY DEAREST MICHAEL

Dearest Michael,

I have been avoiding you and avoiding writing this letter. I recently realized it is because I am angry. I am angry with you. I don't want to be but I am. I love and cherish you so very much! You were such a remarkable human being. How could you ever imagine that life would be better without you? I realize this is not the thought process you were experiencing, and rather you were trying to avoid and stop your pain in the only way you thought possible. What you didn't realize, nor could you possibly understand, is the amount of suffering and pain you have created by your absence... which I know you would NEVER have wanted.

You were a selfless, gentle, kind, loving, strong, stubborn, determined, driven, and funny young man with a contagious laugh. You always treated me as a sister, and I miss you so very much!

As a mental health professional, I help many people walk through their journey with grief and tragedy. I know what to expect, I know what to look for, I know the warning signs and symptoms. And yet, grief can even take professionals by surprise.

You are loved. You are cherished. And you will never be forgotten. You are a part of our family and talked about often. Our children know you, even though they never had the pleasure of meeting you. Your picture hangs on our living room wall along with many other family members. Thank you for loving me unconditionally. Thank you for respecting me. Thank you for protecting and cherishing me. You are an exceptional human being and you have changed my life by being in mine.

  With love,

  Your sister Korah

After reading the manuscript of the book you are now reading, I experienced many waves of emotions. Sadness, confusion, frustration, bargaining, and now I find myself in the phase of anger. How could he not know how much he was loved, how much he would be missed, how much he was cherished, how incredibly unique and awesome he was?! He was like no other, a true gift to this world, and he can never be replaced.

It is okay to be angry. It is okay to be sad. It is okay to question "what if?" It is okay to be in denial, or shock. It is okay to feel any and all emotions, especially with grief. Grief is tricky and different for everyone. What we need, when we need it and how we need it, varies for each person. How I process my emotions on my timeline, and the support I need, will be different than how your siblings, parents, or friends process their grief. To anyone reading this, wherever you find yourself on your grief journey, please know it is okay. Be patient with yourself, be kind to and supportive of yourself. As long as you are acknowledging and not avoiding or denying your emotions, you are moving through your grief. Be patient.

A client of mine described grief as feeling like you have been hit by a boulder rolling down a hill. The boulder crushes you, and it is something you have to carry after being run over. The boulder is huge, and heavy, and impossible. Over time the boulder doesn't go away, it doesn't get lighter, but you get stronger! I love this analogy and believe it to be very true. The pain of grief doesn't go away, and it only gets easier because we get stronger. So, hang in there. You *will* get stronger!

If you believe someone in your life is struggling with thoughts of suicide, I would like to include the following advice. This advice is not exclusive, and if you need immediate assistance do not hesitate to contact your nearest emergency center or call the National Suicide Prevention Lifeline at 1-800-273-8255. You can also text them at 741741.

Upon Michael's return from the military, he was different. He was quiet and guarded. I remember asking, even prying, for information about his experiences at war. He would not share, no matter how hard I pressed. I eventually stopped because I could see he wasn't going to give in. I believe the only piece of information I got him to share with me was how to take someone down quickly. I was a bit of a wild spirit and enjoyed wrestling and being playfully aggressive with anyone who would engage with me. So, Michael finally obliged and took me down in about two seconds. I didn't see it coming and was unable to prevent the pain. I don't remember the exact maneuver, but man, was it effective. It was playful banter, we laughed, and he taught me the move and let me practice on him. This is all he would ever share with me.

Warning sign number one: pay attention to individuals who refuse to talk about their trauma and go to great lengths to cover it up or avoid it. We cannot force someone to talk; however, the stronger they avoid and refuse is an indication of the level of pain they are trying to hide and escape. This does not mean that everyone is going to share all of their pain with everyone. But we do need *someone*, anyone, to share the burden, to share the pain, and make our journey more bearable. We are not intended to endure extreme suffering alone; it is too difficult.

If you suspect someone is avoiding talking or processing their trauma, gently inquire with their loved ones and collaborate. Through a kind, loving, and respectful lens we can inquire about the wellbeing of another. For example, I could have reached out to Michael's mother and asked her how she thought Michael was doing upon his return and if he was sharing any of his stories from the war with her. I could have continued to encourage Michael to talk and remind him that even if I could not relate or possibly understand his suffering and what he experienced, it would not change my opinion or love for him. No matter what he endured, or had to do while at war, I would have supported him unconditionally, without question. He needed to know this, and I failed him. I'm sorry, Michael.

Warning sign number two: Michael started drinking heavily. We were both in our early 20's and engaged in social drinking with friends. Upon Michael's return, however, his drinking became extreme. He would become so heavily intoxicated that he would fall over, pass out, or begin acting out of character. This was not Michael. There appeared to be very little self-control when alcohol was involved. Substance use and abuse are a common warning sign that our loved one is hurting and may be contemplating suicide. Again, I could have approached Michael in a kind, loving, respectful manner and expressed my concern for his behaviors, but I didn't. For this I am sorry, Michael. I loved you too much to not say anything and now it is too late. We all have demons and secrets we are ashamed of. We have all failed and let others down. We have all disappointed others and made mistakes. You were not alone in these feelings and experiences.

Sadly, instead of offering additional support and encouragement to Michael, I stopped hanging around him. I could not bear the sight of him heavily intoxicated. It broke my heart. I moved out of state and we lost touch. My love for him never changed but we were not in contact. From this point forward, I did not know how he was doing, and did not see any additional warning signs. I am sorry, Michael.

Motivated by my pain and love for Michael, and even grief and guilt for losing contact, I offer this short list of additional common warning signs, and hope you find them helpful. They are not precise 1-to-1 signs of suicidal ideation, but they can be signs and symptoms, nonetheless. In no particular order:

1. Staying preoccupied.

    Similar to substance use, staying busy and occupied ensures we don't have time to think about our trauma and pain. Staying busy to ensure we are not left with idle time provides some control over the pain that can feel unmanageable. This is a distraction and can offer false hope. One can feel in control and believe they are carrying along in life with their trauma neatly tucked away. Sadly, when we avoid dealing with our trauma, we may be able to push through, pretend, or suppress for a while; however, eventually, it catches up with us. It is not sustainable to avoid, neglect, resist, or deny our trauma and our pain. No matter how good we are at hiding it, it will eventually resurface and typically in an explosive manner if we have kept it hidden for a long time. Usually when we reach this point, our pain can feel insurmountable. That is not the reality. However, when we reach this point, it can feel as if we are standing at the bottom of an emotional Mount Everest, defeated and without any other option than to escape.

    If you find yourself in this space, it may feel like you're trying to eat a steak without any teeth. It is possible; however, we need to move slowly, take tiny bites of steak, and make sure we are chewing thoroughly. Start with thinking about/processing/

feeling the least emotional piece of your trauma. Take a small bite of your steak. Eventually, over time, by taking small pieces of our trauma and healing, we will consume the entire steak or process through our entire trauma. We must start small, though, or otherwise we will choke. Seek help from a professional and move slow through your trauma. Have excellent coping skills in place to manage your emotions. And most importantly, no matter how horrific or awful we feel our trauma/pain is, we are not alone. I PROMISE you. Someone, probably not far away, has experienced something similar and is also feeling ashamed, embarrassed, and overwhelmed. You are not alone, and you are NOT defined by this event/experience.

2. Inability to sleep and intrusive nightmares.

This is another warning sign that someone is hurting. Sleep is a time that our subconscious mind takes control. It is a space that we are no longer able to control or manipulate and so often those distressing memories we are fighting so hard to stay hidden, become exposed. Some are unable to sleep while other may sleep excessively. Nightmares can be violent, loud, or disruptive and make sleep near impossible. If you have access to your loved one while they sleep, pay attention. If you are not present while they sleep, simply inquire about how they are sleeping. Sleep problems are a symptom of a deep-rooted issue and will not go away without processing and healing from our trauma. Help is needed. This is not your fault.

You've done nothing wrong and you deserve to be healed and have peace. Yes, I'm talking to you!

3. Family history with suicide.

     Having a relative who has completed suicide increases one's risk level significantly. One would think it would be the opposite; however, sadly, statics prove otherwise. If you are worried about a loved one and uncertain if there is a family history with suicide, again gently inquire with family members or the person directly.

4. Substances.

     Substance use and abuse are a common symptom for those considering suicide. Substance use can be a tempting solution to try and numb our pain and escape the mental and emotional torture one may feel. Sadly, this is temporary and not sustainable, and will make it even more difficult to function efficiently and have a productive, meaningful life. This is a sign of one's reality, a sign of the pain one is trying to escape, avoid, resist and possibly deny.

5. Emotional or dramatic responses to simple situations.

     A simple way to observe if our loved one is hurting and avoiding their pain is by paying attention to how they respond to simple situations. Does their response match the encounter they are experiencing? For example, are they becoming rageful, or a puddle of tears, when they stub their toe, watch a scene from a movie, or when someone cuts them off in the parking lot? Our response to simple situations can be an indication of a deeper-rooted concern that is not being addressed, and pokes its ugly head out momentarily through a trauma cue (something that reminds us of our trauma either directly or indirectly/consciously or subconsciously). The more often this happens, or the more intense their response to these trauma cues, is an indication of the pain they are experiences.

6. Self-harm.

When our trauma that we have neatly tucked away begins to expose itself, again it can feel overwhelming and insurmountable. We find ourselves again at the bottom of the emotional Mount Everest. Engaging in acts that provide physical pain is a way for some to escape the emotional pain. This is a symptom of inner pain and needing help. This is a temporary solution to a much larger issue and is not sustainable or effective. It does not help one heal from their trauma it is a temporary solution from a situation/experience that can feel impossible.

7. Isolation/retreat from others physically or emotionally.

If our loved one is isolating from others, physically or emotionally, it is their attempt to try to control or manipulate their feelings. It is an attempt to gain control and mastery over that emotional Mount Everest. Sadly, this is not effective, and often means that in order to manage and control their emotional pain, our loved one becomes more withdrawn or isolated with time. This again is a symptom of their pain.

8. Saying goodbye, and/or giving away belongings.

    This is not something all victims of suicide do; however, it can be a sign. If your loved one has any of the above-mentioned symptoms and then suddenly calls you or shows up and is giving you their items or saying goodbye, pay attention. Typically, these conversations are more discrete and do not usually involve our loved one coming out and directly saying goodbye. The person may be making amends for prior behaviors, apologizing for any pain they have caused you, or for embarrassing you. This may also be done with physically giving away their belongings, or taking care of their possessions in an attempt to make less work for their loved one after they depart. I've worked with people who have killed their own animals in effort to prepare for suicide. This can be a more challenging sign to monitor but simply pay attention and get help immediately if you notice this sign in your loved one.

9. Sudden drastic change in mood.

    This one often goes hand in hand with number eight. If our loved one is typically sad, mad, isolated, depressed, etc. and then one day their mood is DRASTICALLY different and uplifted, this requires immediate attention. This is a sign I look for often as a therapist, and can mean that someone is close to completing suicide. What our loved one is telling/

showing us is that they are at peace with their decision and will follow through with their decision soon. Their decision to end their life provides them with peace, or even excitement... their pain will cease soon. This is so hard because we can be easily fooled to believe they have turned a corner, are feeling better, or are having a good day. After all, this is what we have been hoping for, praying for, and wanting so desperately for our loved one. If the change is drastic, it can be dangerous. If the change is more gradual it can mean they are processing and healing. There is a significant difference.

10. Hopelessness.

This is a significant warning sign. In the therapeutic setting, this is one I pay extremely close attention to. If someone has lost hope, they have very little to fight for, and are more likely to give up and attempt or complete suicide. No matter how awful or horrible our pain/trauma may feel, there is purpose. Each life matters, and is equally amazing. I believe we all have unique talents and skills and need one another. When we lose hope, we lose sight of our purpose and meaning in life. If your loved one has lost hope, remind them of how amazing they are, how loved they are, and how they make this world better. You can also ask them directly the reason they are still alive... what keeps them fighting, what breathes life into their soul, what is worth fighting for? This can help remind our loved one of their own personal hope, and keep them in the fight for life.

If you are watching a loved one suffer and feel helpless, I also encourage you to seek professional help. I know I am biased as a therapist; however, having someone you can talk to about what you are experiencing can offer support, encouragement and hope for you, too. It can be incredibly painful to watch someone we love self-destruct and you should not be alone either in this journey.

No matter how skilled, or how much we love someone, if they are not ready to change, we cannot make them. The best thing we can do is walk alongside this person we love, remind them how much they are loved (unconditionally – regardless of their mistakes and trauma), remind them we will not judge them or ask probing questions, and we will always be there for them. We cannot change someone; it is an impossible task. You are also not responsible for their actions, good or bad. If you suspect someone is hurting, it is ok to ask them direct questions and inquire if they are having thoughts of suicide. Bring the elephant in the room. Let them know you care, and you're not afraid to talk about difficult things. A professional therapist can also help you navigate this conversation, as I realize this may be a tall order.

Michael, what you may not know is that I too struggled with depression and thoughts of suicide. I felt completely hopeless, alone, sad, scared, and overwhelmed. Our emotions were the result of different experiences-nonetheless, equally devastating. I did everything I could to stop the pain, but nothing worked and suicide felt like the only option. Fast forwarding now twenty years, I see and understand that my pain had meaning. I endured that pain for a reason, for a greater cause. I am able to better relate to those I work with who are suffering from trauma, depression,

PTSD, and thoughts of suicide. I was so close to ending my life, and I am so glad I didn't. I have a purpose. You had a purpose, and your life continues to have a purpose. You changed me and made me better. You taught me so much about life and friendship. You will always be loved, and you will always be missed. You are a part of frequent conversations in our house and our children know you.

I am no longer angry with Michael and have moved on to forgiveness. I understand the pain he must have felt in order to consider suicide as an option. I've been there, I can relate and my heart breaks for him.

Thank you for loving me so well, Michael. You will forever be missed and loved!

Korah & Michael

For some, I know, circumstances following the loss of a loved one can be very complicated. And so, I will now share the rest of our story.

CHAPTER 10

COMPLICATION

In our case, the aftermath of Michael's death came with great and unpleasant personal and legal complications, which I will not entirely detail here. I offer this chapter for those who may also face the difficult, complicated aftermath of losing a loved one.

Unfortunately, this can occur at a time when you're least mentally and emotionally able to handle an outer world struggle. Inwardly, you're busy fighting to keep your head above water.

Legal Matters

The death of a loved one should bring people together. Often, sadly, it pulls them apart.

I never understood the importance of a will until we lost Michael. When there's a will, it's important to follow it immediately; refer to it before making any final arrangements.

In the case of military personnel, there should always be a will. The military requires each member to create one prior to deployment.

We remembered the will too late, and as a result, Michael was already cremated when that was not in his will at all. Michael had expressed in recent years he preferred to be cremated. It's cheaper. A traditional burial can be very expensive. I sincerely felt he still preferred to be buried in his hometown as stated in his will. Michael was sensible, and his reasoning behind cremation was financial. At the time of his death, I was in a weakened state; that was how events played out. The truth is, both sides involved in this conflict were emotionally overwhelmed.

Be aware, too, that once the deceased's estate hits probate court, the focus is on their estate. It's about "stuff." Probate's focus is on the monetary value of things, bank and investment accounts, material items, funeral expenses.

By the time my mother recalled that Michael had given her papers to be stored in her safe, it was already too late. Among those papers was the will Michael had written right before deploying to Iraq that could have made things clearer. I say clearer, but not easier; the narrative was being directed, and it wasn't by me. I couldn't think straight or get anything right. Not Kristina either. I must add; she cared only for Michael, not for the things they had amassed together. She was willing to forfeit any and all possessions. Among a host of other issues, we had conflicting ideas on how to honor Michael's final wishes, including his final resting place.

Personally, I didn't care about things. I just wanted my son buried in his hometown because I felt that was what he would want, and I desperately wanted to bring him home. I wanted Michael out of Kentucky, the wretched place where he killed himself. I just wanted him to rest in peace.

There is another important reason to know and to abide by the terms of a will. If the will is broken, in the eyes of a probate judge, all bets are off.

I was named executor to Michael's will. Accusations of deliberately disregarding the will proceeded. It wasn't true. I was in shock–I forgot. Michael had mentioned cremation when my husband expressed that he wanted to be cremated. Michael said, "Me, too. It makes more sense."

The legal argument about Michael's remains proceeded in court. If Michael had changed his mind about being buried in a casket *versus* cremation, he could very well have changed his mind about his final resting place. This is an unusual case in that it was not only about property, money, and funeral expenses; it was about Michael's cremains and his final resting spot.

I wanted to bring him home, as he expressed in the will; others prefer he be buried in Arlington National Cemetery. If Michael had wanted to be buried in Arlington Cemetery, he would have and could have expressed that in his will. After all, he was serving in the military when it was written. Michael didn't even stand for military recognition at his own graduation. I thought that spoke volumes. I was totally against Arlington. Now I'll continue to carry that heavy burden of making such a vital mistake.

The idea of burying Michael in Arlington came out of nowhere. Not just anyone can be buried there. I thought it was a bizarre request, and I wondered if he qualified for burial there. It honestly didn't matter to me since I just wanted to bring him home.

In the previous chapter, I mentioned that, despite pressure, I felt highly uneasy about signing the paper to have Michael cremated. My focus was on getting Michael blessed and buried. Because I ignored my intuition and signed the paper, the judge had no sympathy for any other requests I made because I had already violated the will. I have had a hard time forgiving myself for that mistake.

Our case was deadlocked. The judge expressed if we couldn't agree, she would split the ashes between us. I didn't want that. Instead, she decided to order mediation.

Dealing With the Veterans Administration

The V.A. can be helpful. And – as too many vets can attest – it can be a nightmare to deal with at times, like any bureaucracy. The never-ending paperwork is exhausting and, in a way, insulting, as you're jumping through endless hoops to obtain what rightfully belongs to a veteran and/or their family after loyal service.

In our case, the V.A. denied death benefits because this was a case of suicide. The insult here is that the V.A. is unable to help the number of veterans returning from combat who are suffering from post-traumatic stress disorder, then denies death benefits to the families of those who die by suicide when they could not get help from the government that had no problem exposing them to the stresses and horrors of war. As a result, as of this writing, some *twenty-two veterans a day commit suicide*. This is both a great tragedy, *and* the lack of resources to help them and their families is a travesty.

I'd sent the V.A. a video, with Michael stating in his own words, "There isn't a day that goes by that I don't think about that crash and those that didn't make it home alive!" In fact, I had to send them three CDs, because they lost the first two. His best friend, Erik, sent a heartfelt letter, testifying that Michael confided he knew he was suffering from PTSD. All of it was dismissed.

After I'd learn the gruesome details from the horrific events in Iraq, I'd imagined Michael working alongside his brothers immediately following the helicopter crash, scouring the hold, looking for more decaying remains. What Michael witnessed was a gruesome scene; comrades were annihilated. They were only able to find the smallest of body parts, fingers, and toes. They were scattered everywhere. For days after, they flew over that hole in the ground, the final resting spot of his friends, his brothers-in-arms. All the while, he kept thinking of the rookie aircrew Chief he'd assigned, who had left a wife and five young children. I can't imagine the effects of viewing this horrific crash, let alone the anguish from that fateful decision.

I must say, knowing what I know now about dealing with the V.A., I am not surprised that Michael didn't seek help from them. Their solutions, I have learned, usually involve a handful of pills, an ineffective antidote to "helping" veterans seeking help – a "solution" that can in some cases make a bad situation worse because pills are only a Band-Aid over a mortal wound.

I knew beyond a doubt that the long shadow I'd witnessed falling deeper and deeper over his mind and soul, despite his heroic efforts to go on, was indeed a result of PTSD. Eventually, this shadow took him.

I can't imagine the circumstances the V.A. requires a combat veteran to suffer before they will arrive at this diagnosis.

What to Do if You Involve the V.A.

Be aware: Once a claim is filed with the V.A., it takes time and patience because their response can involve a long, drawn-out process. Don't count on funds from a burial benefit. Or, if you're among the few approved, they won't be available to help immediately.

In the case of suicide, PTSD must be documented and diagnosed by a qualified medical professional in order to seek benefits. Brace yourself for denial and unending paperwork. Be prepared to file an appeal. You may need to seek organizations and/or attorneys who are willing and able to accompany veterans and their families; some are able to work *pro bono*.

Keep in mind you are not alone. The struggles you face regarding claims are shared, unfortunately, by numerous veterans and their families. Don't waver; there's strength in numbers. Personal struggles involving Michael's estate prompted my decision to drop the appeal. I needed a sense of closure and time to heal.

Personal or Family Conflicts

In our case, it was necessary to take legal action in order to obtain Michael's ashes. The conflict started long before the probate court, but the case needed to be settled, and, as mentioned above, the judge ordered mediation.

If you can't afford the expense of an attorney and court fees, seek help from a mediation service. I want to add: if at all possible, avoid legal action, because it can be extremely expensive. A mediator can be less expensive, keeping in mind that each party pays half.

Parties in disagreement must agree. Thankfully, our mediator came highly recommended and demonstrated compassion; his lifetime of experience was key as he guided us. He also graciously provided his service at no cost. That's unheard of, and a blessing I'll never forget. His service could've easily cost upwards of thousands of dollars given the great deal of time he spent. Both parties had lawyers present, so we really weren't saving other than what the mediator could have demanded; after all, it was court-ordered.

The fact is, the legal papers you need to close an estate can be filed on your own. However, if you're not familiar with probate or legal process, you can make costly mistakes. State rules and regulations vary.

For example, Kentucky – where Michael and Kristina lived – has no common law. That became one of our biggest obstacles; otherwise, Kristina would have been in charge and entitled to everything. Rightfully so, in my opinion.

In order to keep costs down, avoid attorney emails and calls. When you schedule a legal consultation, consolidate questions. Search for answers on your own first. My probate legal fees escalated to well over eleven thousand dollars. This was an unusual case even for the seasoned attorney I worked with. He tried his best to keep my legal fees under control. The monetary value of Michael's estate was nowhere near what the legal fees and funeral expenses added up to. He was just getting started, fresh out of college. My objective was to get Michael's cremains and bury him in his hometown. Nothing else really mattered.

If you decide legal action is necessary, I highly recommend that you count the cost before making a move. Legal action is always costly, if not in terms of the cash needed, then in terms of the emotional expense.

Before our mediation process, I had second thoughts about proceeding. I couldn't take any more. It had been five months since Michael's death, and I wanted just to bury his ashes and go on with life. I needed to let go of the control, the stronghold, which felt like a losing battle. At the same time, how do you walk away from honoring your son and his final wishes?

My attorney said, "We've come so far. Let's give mediation a try."

I knew in my gut it wouldn't be that simple. Unfortunately, neither party was willing to compromise on a final resting place. Stepping away from a legal process was not an option.

The mediation finally occurred, not without last-minute drama. My attorney insisted I could do this by phone. When I double-checked at the last minute, he had learned that I needed to be there in person. It wasn't going to happen, not last minute. I didn't live around the corner. Besides, I'd already traveled to Kentucky. The expense was taking a toll, not to mention each time I left bewildered and broken.

With a lot of coaxing from my attorney and the mediator, we did get the job done by phone. It was exhausting and grueling, lasting into the evening hours, taking way longer than it should have.

In the end, I bore much more than any parent should ever endure to honor my son in the way he had stated in his will. (Go back and review the importance of a will and knowing where it is.)

Back to Our Story – In the End

Per our mediation agreement, I set a date for the interment. There were more complications which, again, I will not detail here. Suffice to say, it was terrible. I had additional roadblocks that were emotionally exhausting for me.

It was now the end of May, and Michael had passed away the previous September. I desperately wanted Michael buried before Mothers' Day or Memorial Day – definitely before he and Kristina's wedding date, which would have been the upcoming July 4th.

One week before Michael and Kristina's scheduled wedding, Michael's remains were laid to rest in his hometown of Johnson City, New York, on June 27, 2015 – National PTSD Awareness Day.

Somehow, I felt that my mission, to reach out and help others, was just beginning.

As I bring the main portion of this book to close, I hope that reading about my experiences and what I learned has helped you.

Twenty-two veterans die by suicide every day. That is a staggering number. We need to own this. There is strength in numbers, and we must unite to put an end to this tragedy. PTSD is real and can be deadly. It isn't going to go away by ignoring it.

I'd much rather be reading this passage than writing it. If Michael was still alive, I'd have time to be proactive. Having said that, I feel a responsibility to share. There are other mothers and fathers, sisters and brothers, husbands and wives out there who know their loved one is struggling. For many, it's not too late.

Work as hard as you can to get them help. Survivor's guilt and war trauma can choke the life out of someone. Its devastating grip is hard to escape, but with help, it can be done.

The circumstances surrounding our ordeal were surreal. I survived it, and I still have a hard time grasping it. Michael is gone. When the reality sank in, it became less about his departure and more about his choice of destinations: death was somehow more appealing than being part of this world and our family. Seeking help wasn't an option. Why?

Unfortunately, Michael's life went full circle. He was born amid turbulence. When he died, a whirlwind of emotional turmoil erupted. Truthfully, I find it sad and a bit ironic considering how kind and accommodating he was. The circumstances that welcomed him and the way he left us are far from defining who and what he represented in the thirty-two and a half years in between.

His suicide triggered life-changing destruction.

We'd endured blustery health obstacles, weather-beaten and worn from surgeries and catastrophic natural disasters. None compare to the devastation of his loss. I'd continued down Survivor's Guilt Lane until my journey came to a complete halt; it's not natural to stop living when you're still alive.

I've learned the hard way that exposure is paramount. Sunny days are fine. We all enjoy nice weather, but the forecast isn't always sunny. We should prepare for storms. Had I fully known the details surrounding Michael's war experiences, I could have and would have been better prepared. I should have been exposed to those ugly hard truths.

As for my intuition, it was real and spot on. I will never ignore my intuition again.

For me, grief was an unfamiliar emotion. I don't think you can fully understand survivor's guilt unless you've experienced it. I understand. I get it- the military parental consent, missed cues, forgetting the will, the cremation- I'd pretty much failed on every level both in his life and death. I suffered from survivor's guilt. I ventured down the same dark road Michael traveled; I needed to change direction. I turned to help. It's out there, sometimes where you least except it.

Strength grew. It developed from those who'd profoundly suffered. Military members, some that loved Michael dearly, others he'd never met. Mothers, some who lost children like myself, threw me a lifeline right as I was going under; somehow, they knew.

When you survive suicide, you bear the burden of not stopping this tragic event. Survivor's guilt can't be ignored; you need to face it, reason with it. I found the courage to seek forgiveness. After a suicide, someone needs forgiveness. Perhaps for those that left us, others may feel it was those that surrounded them, our loved ones. For me, it was myself.

And my forgiveness didn't stop there.

The door to Catholicism may as well have been slammed in my face. After I wittnessed a "suicide is damned to hell" sermon. I hit rock bottom in a Florida church pew, then my regular place of worship. I reached out to another pastor nearby. Not every Catholic priest gave up on Michael, or me, for that matter. I was embraced with open arms and an open heart, and a completely different attitude, one that included forgiveness and mercy. I still attend Mass to this day.

Michael made me proud. His success could be calculated in the wisdom he accumulated. He'd accomplished so many achievements yet was modestly humble. He had a stellar military record, a prestigious air medal, alongside several meritorious mast awards. I prefer to chronicle his legacy by the way he lived a leader, loyal and faithful. He treated others with respect and dignity regardless of circumstance.

Having said that, I refuse to let Michael's final act define him; my son was a kind, compassionate soul. He was passionate about giving back and helping others. His good deeds were accompanied by unconditional love. How can I beat myself up for raising such a wonderful young man?

It took a long time before I realized I couldn't let his final act define me, either. He couldn't have possibly been loved or adored more; he was my definition of pride and joy.

I'll keep moving forward. My motivation is honoring Michael and other veterans suffering from PTSD. I made a conscious decision to navigate beyond that painful intersection. In doing so, I'm honored to share a small piece of Michael's life and death. I hope and pray Michael's story can somehow help halt the staggering number of veterans' suicides. If we can save one life, then Michael's death was not in vain. Let this be a lesson for us all; no man or woman comes home from war unscathed.

Michael suffered in silence; it's time to break that silence. Every veteran suffering with PTSD deserves to be heard. Let Michael's story be the voice for so many veterans still living in silence.

Michael gave so much of himself in life; I have confidence his story will continue that legacy.

In order to finish my account of these events, however, I must tell you about an experience that occurred after Michael's burial. What I have to share may not be for everyone – I caution you, especially if you are a religious traditionalist– but it gave me a measure of comforting hope, and perhaps it will help you, too.

EPILOGUE

MICHAEL WALKS WITH ME

During the months between Michael's death and his interment, I lived in inner turmoil and darkness. Despite the gorgeous weather, I existed in a cloudy, poignant sadness.

Four long months after Michael's death, I was sitting on our lanai in the sunshine beside our pool. I was engaged in a usual ritual, saying the rosary.

Despite the warmth and brightness of the day, I felt desperate and surrounded by darkness. I would briefly pause to cry with my hands covering my face.

All I could see was a great looming blackness – a vast space of grief and suffering. Is that where Michael was?

No. That's impossible. Michael was such a good person. Still, my church's teaching about suicide told me he must be in a terrible place of outer darkness. No, not Michael. I needed to stop thinking about this; I couldn't keep letting my mind wander there. It was torture.

As I sat with my face in my hands, suddenly, a beam of energy seemed to engulf me – something I'd never experienced before.

I pulled my hands away and glanced at them. They were trembling, and goosebumps spread up my arm and over my whole body. A powerful and unexplainable energy field was penetrating my dark mood, and I was engulfed in compassion.

In a few moments, the experience subsided – but the memory of it marked me. What was it all about?

Whatever transpired in that moment had forever changed me in that I knew unequivocally it was a spiritual encounter. In an instant, my spirit had been transformed from a place of dark despair and pain to a sanctuary of calm.

When I got up, I realized there was no logical explanation for the profound sense of change that had come over me. How would I explain it? I knew I'd have to be careful who I shared this experience with; after all, my state of mind had been fragile. What would people think?

During this period, Michael's cremains had not been returned to me. How then was everything "alright"?

I would link this experience to something that happened months later, after Michael's interment.

Not everybody will welcome this next part of my story with open arms. Certain friends have outwardly expressed concerns about me seeking a medium, questioning their credibility, while others – conservative Christian people – have questioned morality, saying that it's evil. Still, others have said what I'm about to share is all rubbish. Having said that... this particular encounter turned plenty of doubters into believers!

Personally, I cherish what happened next.

As a parent suffering the loss of a son to suicide, I longed for answers. Many parents that bear such a loss seek out spiritual mediums. It's only natural to check on our children's wellbeing, whether they are here or have gone to the other side. I'm still Michael's mother. I think about him all the time, and I will till the day I die. Nothing's changed in that regard.

My situation was worse, my grief more of torment, perhaps, because I had heard a sermon that shook me to my core. The floor fell beneath my feet as the priest at the podium delivered a sermon that said anyone who has ended their own life is damned to hell for all eternity.

Thankfully, I was relieved by what was, for me, a new kind of spiritual encounter.

Enter, Medium/psychic Denise.

Naturally pure and honest, Denise is a kind and compassionate woman. She cried while sharing the sentiments that came forth during the hour we spent together. Feelings and experiences she could not have known about came out. I knew immediately that her words weren't by chance or a wild guess; they were exact and precise – about things only Nichole and Michael knew.

My first visit with Denise occurred two years after we lost Michael. I'll admit, I had no idea what to expect. I was a nervous wreck, shaking, scared of what I might learn, or worse yet, that there would be no contact at all.

As I entered the room, though, Denise promptly informed me that Michael was there, and in fact, he'd been waiting. Almost immediately, she said he'd taken his own life. She'd described a Naval station and helicopters, along with what she described as pilots in the surrounding area. She thought Michael was in the Navy because she could see large ships in the background.

I corrected her. "No, he's a Marine, but at one point, he was stationed on a Naval ship."

He had a deployment to Japan on a ship, the 31st MEU, which responded to disaster relief.

She immediately stated, "He was in Fallujah around the heaviest fighting of the war. He's telling me that he suffered trauma and depression that started there and became PTSD. He believes that being there was right, that he was on the right side, the right team. In one way, it was a supportive environment. There was a 'hurrah for us' kind of environment."

I thought of the Marine's famous "OO-RAH!" shout.

"No. That wasn't the problem. It was something else."

I held my breath.

"Something terrible happened. In the dark and silence of night when he closed his eyes, he could not stop seeing it. He says, 'When there's no hurrah, you're all alone it's very different. When you're with your soul self, it's not the same.'"

She seemed to be feeling Michael's anguish because tears filled her eyes and her voice trembled.

"Michael says he is so sorry for the mess caused by his death. He says, 'I made a mess of things.' I can tell he's very ashamed for all the pain and torment you've suffered."

My throat was so tight I couldn't respond except to nod.

"The great thing is he has transitioned to the other side. He's adjusting, in heaven, and still healing."

The terrible weight of that condemning sermon lifted from my shoulders, and I began to weep.

"Michael watches you suffer and cry. He says when you're in distress, it's painful to see."

I felt upset again. "How could he be okay in heaven if he feels my pain and knows that his actions caused pain and suffering for me – and for his brother and sister, Kristina, and others, too?"

Denise assured me that in heaven, he has help dealing with that burden.

"Michael is saying he's grateful for the viewing in Kentucky and the services in New York."

How did she know about that?

"I feel awkward about bringing this up for some reason. Was he buried in his military uniform – because he's showing me that?"

That was a clinker.

"NO!" I almost shouted. "But he should have been."

"Strange, she's clearly confused; he's showing me an image of himself in his military uniform, and I'm seeing Arlington National Cemetery, with Marines standing at attention."

I realized what Michael was trying to convey. I have to admit I was shocked!

"Maybe it's a message with a personal meaning. In any case, he's thanking you for all that you've done. He says, 'Thank you for the *services* you did have.'"

I wasn't about to waste time on an explanation. I was thinking, *Wow.* Michael was now thanking me for "bringing him home!"

And then there was the admission that he'd been very broken in spirit – as if he were pleading with me and everyone else to understand why he felt he had to escape the pain. He talked about the grave mistakes he'd felt he made – decisions for which he'd felt responsible during this life, not solely, but enough that the heavy burden of them had crushed out light and life.

"Michael is saying you did nothing wrong – you were a good mother," Denise said. "Michael asked for support, and you supported him. That is what a mother is supposed to do. He would have enlisted with or without your signature. He was born a warrior."

Suddenly, Denise took off in another direction. Michael was describing a young and pretty blonde woman, but that was not Kristina. I realized Denise was describing Michael's former fiancé, who had bright blue eyes and a daughter. I realized as soon as she mentioned the little girl who it was.

So many details were pouring out, I felt overwhelmed.

She changed direction again. "When you see butterflies, do you think of Michael?"

"Yes!" I blurted out. I'd just placed a memorial tree in my family room, complete with butterflies. They reminded me of spirit and light and life.

"Well, Michael is showing me butterflies. He says you're thinking about getting a tattoo – perhaps a butterfly?"

My jaw fell open. I'd never liked tattoos, but I'd been contemplating getting one – of a beautiful butterfly – to remind me of Michael, this beautiful son who had lived for too short a time on this earth and who left behind so many lovely memories.

"This is unusual," Denise veered off again, but this time she looked perplexed. "Michael showing me something Egyptian. A vivid image of a mummy in a gold-trimmed tomb."

I almost fell over. My coworker Yenisey and I were working on an Egyptian tomb with a mummy, helping her sister complete a school project.

I could tell Denise knew what was going on as she continued to describe what we were making. She finished with, "I believe this is his way of letting you know he's still with you. He's around you!"

Later, when I mentioned this to Yenisey, she was downright shocked. She reminded me that once when we were stymied, she'd asked Michael for help, right out loud. Her exact words were, "Michael. I don't know what to do, come on, help me out here!" I had done the same, thinking the task seemed more difficult than we could handle– and that maybe someone on the other side could assist. "We need Michael's help for this one!" Ever the creative one, he had enjoyed molding and creating things. Michael had been there with us! When we called for help, he was there.

Again, I was bowled over. How could Denise, a stranger, know details that only Yenisey and I were aware of? I was glad Yenisey was a witness and that she had taken a photo of what we worked on – recording down to the last detail Denise described. "You used a shiny gold paint."

After that, Denise talked at great lengths about Michael's brothers-in-arms. Michael expressed awareness of the kind acts Erik was involved in. She mentioned a fundraiser he'd sponsored to help us with our piling legal fees, raising about $2,600. He also worked hard on Michael's behalf, progressively helping veteran causes, participating in many bike races, some honoring Michael.

"Michael says, 'Tell him thank you for everything.'"

After discussing Erik, Denise asked, "Who's Steve?"

Of course, she was referring to Michael's brother, my other son.

"Michael says, 'Say hello to Steve.'" He went on asking that I convey personal messages to both Steve and his sister, Nichole.

Denise said, "Now he's showing me Robin Williams."

Just a couple of weeks before Michael's death, I had talked with him about Robin Williams' suicide. At that time, Michael had seemed to condone Robin's decision. Once I had gathered a little composure, it was one of the first things I'd thought about after Michael passed away. It was a warning sign – and I wished I'd understood that then.

The message to me was that I couldn't have known then what I know now. Michael had been good about covering his emotional state for everyone. He'd kept busy and seemed to focus on future events. Even he had not known that this was an avoidance tactic, a way to distract himself from those dark clouds that were mounting and blocking out his inner light.

He'd saved Nichole and Kristina for last, it seemed. He knew he'd disappointed them the most. Everything he said for Nichole was indisputable but very personal and will remain private.

He was deeply sad and ashamed for hurting Kristina. No words could express how he felt. He was aware of how his actions profoundly affected her. He knew the earth had fallen out from beneath her feet – how she'd been physically ill for days and days after learning of his death. He could not have been sorrier. "There was no way she could have known how bad I was feeling inside. She could not have prevented what I did."

After that session, I didn't plan to see Denise again. There was no need; I could talk to Michael anytime. But I wound up going back some months later to accompany Kari, a friend who had also lost her middle son Michael "Mickey" many years earlier. All three of our children graduated from high school together. I had to share this exceptional experience with her; after all, she was a big part of my support system. She was planning a trip to Florida. We scheduled back-to-back appointments.

Denise, "Michael is here. He's been waiting, knowing you'd come back. First, he says, '*You are a good mother*. I couldn't have asked for a better one. Mom- you did nothing wrong! You need to know that. I love you.' Michael immediately started opening a door, and there's vast darkness beyond it – sheer blackness. I'm not sure why he's showing me this." She paused. "*Why, Michael?*"

Suddenly, she turned to me. "Did you ever wonder about his spirit's journey? Were you thinking about this? Were you asking about this?"

"Yes," I answered quickly.

My mind flew back to the afternoon months before when, seated by our pool at home, I had sensed a great and terrible darkness and feared that his soul was stuck there as my church taught. "He's showing me that despair and darkness had surrounded him." Denise said it was self-imposed. He didn't have to go to this place, Denise carefully explained. "This is a place suicides sometimes go, but not always. It's not a pleasant place. It holds pain and suffering similar to an insane asylum. It's a place of self-punishment. Michael doesn't want to be there, and he wants you to know he realizes he didn't belong there anymore.

"He is telling me he has the faith and courage to reach out to God. He's asking God for help. I can hear him saying, 'God, please don't leave me here!'"

I was choking up, thinking that Michael was not abandoning the faith with which he'd been raised.

"I see three Marines entering into this unpleasant place now," Denise said, her voice full of awe. "They appear to be pilots because they're wearing headgear. They've come to get Michael. He's showing us that he is being saved from his own self-punishment and despair."

I began to shake and cry.

Denise said, "I'm getting goosebumps!"

Denise was crying, too, as we shared tears of relief and joy.

His brothers-in-arms did not abandon him even on the other side. No Marine was left behind.

Erik pointed out sending in three Marines was significant since every mission requires a team made up of four. Two pilots and two aircrew, Michael reunited with his brothers-in-arms, making it a full team. I had no doubt fellow Marines came. I had never once given up hope; in turn, faith never gave up on Michael. Nor did his comrades.

In that instant, Michael's countenance transformed. Light and healing energy flooded in.

Hope filled me, and I whispered to myself.

After that spiritual encounter, I thought he was safe; I know he is safe now.

This experience was essential to share here at the end of this book because with it came much-needed solace. The positive impact was life-changing. My views on death drastically transformed; somehow, life and death are harmoniously integrated.

I'm no expert; I have no answers, only experiences. This life experience will forever be treasured — unforgettable and tattooed on my soul.

Like a beautiful butterfly – a symbol of resurrection.

Tattoo by: Jenna Boyter

Dear Michael,

I witnessed the calm before the storm...

Despite the silence—I'd been warned.
You screamed for help;

I did not know - mounting darkness
would continue to grow.

I'd been hit by this storm, then buried
alive, incapable, unable to thrive.

Somehow.... Strength grew from deep
within. A faithful journey was about to
begin.

I promised to hold a Veteran's hand,

After all, it was my initial plan.

Yet, somehow six years slipped away.

I'm grateful that I can finally say....

There isn't anything I wouldn't do if
only I could've saved you.

Forgiving myself set you free. It's
liberating for both you and me.

At last, you can rest in peace as my self-
destruction starts to ease.

I'm ready to lite that torch to share,

Of post-traumatic stress to bear.

If one Veteran can overcome pain,

I'll know you died not in vain.

May God bless America and all those
who have served.

With Love and pride,

Mom

RESOURCES

Alliance of Hope
https:/allianceofhope.org/find-support/

Flourish Center for Cultivating Human Potential
Korah Hoffman, Clinical Social work/Therapist, LMSW, MPA
www.flourishhumanity.com
328 E Main Street
Spring Arbor, MI 49283
Phone: 517-645-3033

Grief Support for Suicide Loss Survivors
https:/save.org/what-we-do/grief-support

Psychic/Medium Denise Lescano
https/deniselescano.com
9220 Bonita Beach Rd SW
Bonita Springs, Florida 34134
Phone: 239-405-9591

Tragedy Assistance Program for Survivors (TAPS)
https://www.taps.org
800-959-TAPS (8277)

Suicide Support Groups

https:/suicide.supportgroups.com

US Department of Veteran's Affairs

810 Vermont Ave NW,

Washington DC 20420

https:/www.vagov/

Veteran's Transition and Resource Center VTRC

https://www.veteransresourcecenter.org/

Wounded Warrior Project

Veteran's Resource center: 888-997-2586

https:/woundedwarriorproject.org

ABOUT THE AUTHOR

This memoir was born from a tragic experience no one should ever have to confront, or face alone. It's not a story I want to share, rather one that needs to be heard. I feel a responsibility to "tell our story." My mission is to speak out for those who suffer in silence like Michael. I'll be a voice for those struggling with PTSD.

I was excited, downright elated, to have Michael home from war, fully intact, safe and sound. That mindset was a vital mistake… no man or women returns from war unscathed.

My passion is fueled by pain. Twenty-two Veterans die daily by suicide; it's a heartbreaking statistic that is unbearable and unacceptable. Once you've read this book, please, pass it on… awareness is essential for change!